ↄ

Who Elected the Bankers?

A volume in the series
Cornell Studies in Political Economy
Edited by Peter J. Katzenstein

❧

Who Elected the Bankers?

Surveillance and Control in the World Economy

❧

Louis W. Pauly

❧

Cornell University Press
Ithaca and London

Library of Congress Cataloging-in-Publication Data

Pauly, Louis W.
    Who elected the bankers? : surveillance and control in the
world economy / Louis W. Pauly.
        p.   cm. — (Cornell studies in political economy)
    Includes bibliographical references and index.
    ISBN 0-8014-3322-3 (cloth : alk. paper)
    ISBN 0-8014-8375-1 (pbk. : alk. paper)
    1. Financial institutions, International—History—20th
century. 2. League of Nations—History—20th century.
3. International Monetary Fund—History—20th century.
I. Title. II. Series.
HG3881.P34   1997
332.1'5—DC21   95-42066

First published 1997 by Cornell University Press
First printing, Cornell Paperbacks, 1998

Printed in the United States of America

Cornell University Press strives to use environmentally responsible suppliers and materials to the fullest extent possible in the
publishing of its books. Such materials include vegetable-based,
low-VOC inks and acid-free papers that are recycled, totally
chlorine-free, or partly composed of nonwood fibers.

Cloth printing   10 9 8 7 6 5 4 3 2 1

Paperback printing   10 9 8 7 6 5 4 3 2

For my parents,
Louis W. Pauly, Sr., and Elizabeth A. Pauly

Contents

Preface

HARDLY A DAY PASSES THAT WE ARE NOT REMINDED OF AN EMERGING global economy. Nearly every day, it seems, we learn about the expansion of some multinational corporate behemoth. Nearly every day, we hear that international traders are pummeling the currency of some country because they don't like the national "balance sheet." Nearly every day, the workers of the next generation are being warned to expect a significant degree of mobility in their careers and to develop the flexible skills required for competitive success in global markets.

For the vast majority of us who are not Wall Street coupon clippers, not thrilled by the prospect of changing employment fields six or seven times in the course of our lifetime, and not particularly interested in moving to Singapore, this news about "globalization" engenders a deep sense of disquiet. We wonder exactly what we are gaining, and we fear for what we may be losing.

The distemper of any particular age has many sources. An underlying source of our own uneasiness surely lies in the palpably heightening tension between international economic integration and the practical possibilities of national politics. That tension poses an ever more obvious challenge to the very legitimacy of our contemporary political order. This book concerns that challenge.

Markets for money are now commonly depicted as the most global of all markets—and the harbinger of things to come. The claim is exaggerated, but there is something to it. Indeed, for most countries and for most of the world's people, the ebbs and flows of freer movements of international capital are now associated with profound political and social change.

Most fundamentally, the integration of the world's capital markets throws into question the way in which raw political power is transformed into legitimate authority. Today, that transformation is accomplished by structures and processes that we associate with the state. The further financial integration proceeds, however, the more it becomes apparent that truly global capital markets pose a threat to the legitimacy of the state itself. Citizens already hear ever more frequently that there is nothing the leaders of their states can do about this or that pressing domestic problem, because the workings of increasingly integrated capital markets leave no room for maneuver. If such claims are true, they make the threat plain. This book explores the threat posed to political legitimacy in an age of deepening international financial integration. In this regard, it underlines important distinctions among particular states and focuses principally on the leading industrial democracies.

Increasingly integrated capital markets have not grown mysteriously out of some forgotten seed planted long ago. Rather, they reflect deliberate decisions and policy choices made over many years by sovereign states, and especially by powerful states. I do not aim to provide a comprehensive introduction to the arcana of international monetary and financial politics. Instead, my central aim is to explicate, in as nontechnical a language as possible, the forces behind the development of well-known but little understood institutions that now stand at the intersection of international finance and national politics.

The International Monetary Fund is emblematic of a set of formal and informal institutions, ranging from the Group of Seven to the Organization for Economic Cooperation and Development, that now exist at that intersection. My economist friends write paper after paper exploring the technical intricacies of what the IMF and its analogs actually do on a daily basis. My project is cast at a more general level. Concentrating on the International Monetary Fund and a long-forgotten antecedent, I locate the underlying rationale for such institutions in the dilemma of political legitimacy—a dilemma that has become increasingly apparent. Analogs to the IMF are discussed, but I emphasize the evolution of the core mandate of the IMF as it relates to the basic interests of advanced industrial states. Much related research focuses on the relationship between the IMF and less developed countries. Although I rely on much of that work, the dilemma in which I am interested here is firmly embedded in relations among the leading states themselves. International institutions often appear to be ephemeral to those interests, but appearances are deceiving. The closer we get to a world of truly global finance, the more central they become—not because they must inevitably usurp the political authority of states, but because they help states address their deepening legitimacy problem.

There was a time, between the two world wars, when some dreamed of restoring the global capital markets that had existed before 1914. Into that dream, they drew a most unlikely political institution—the League of Nations. The questions why they did so, and to what effect, are relevant to our own time, when once again some are dreaming about—or fearing—a world of global finance. The dilemma of political legitimacy in our world is deepening quickly, but it is not new.

Specialists in international relations and international political economy will find other reasons to be interested in the links between the League and the IMF. I have deliberately kept the text concise and tried not to encumber it with unnecessary detail, but some colleagues will see in those links a new pathway to research on the reciprocal interaction of international economics and domestic politics. Others will draw a connection to research currently exploring the role of specialized, knowledge-based communities in fostering international cooperation and promoting institutional innovation. Without bogging down in theory and technicalities, the book calls attention to a commonsensical train of thought that is often submerged in scholarly debates over "social learning." The argument runs like this: learning requires teachers; the best teachers have experience to share; experience matters when the present is actually not as different from the past as it seems; longevity and open-mindedness in teachers are definite assets; and an institutional base is important to preserve a collective memory of lessons learned. In this light, the book demonstrates that some of the parallels between the League and the Fund are neither coincidental nor circumstantial. For specialists interested in drawing out this and other themes, an extensive set of notes follows the text. For nonspecialists, I have appended a list of suggested follow-up readings.

This book is a work of synthesis, but not just of related themes from a number of fields of study. I think of it as a modest tapestry that weaves together several threads of my own life. Dominick Salvatore, Eugene Diulio, Richard Levich, and Ingo Walter introduced me to international economics and finance many years ago, at Fordham University and New York University. The fathers of the Society of Jesus, who opened the world of philosophy and political theory to me at Fordham, passed on the compelling idea that markets, no matter how well they work, can never be ends in themselves. Shortly thereafter, at the London School of Economics and Political Science, Susan Strange personified the linkage implied by the school's name and piqued my interest in the political forces at work beneath international financial markets. A few years later at Cornell University, Peter Katzenstein nurtured that interest and challenged me to cross ever more firmly entrenched disciplinary boundaries. In between, and just after those years spent in the groves of academe, I had the good fortune to work in the rapidly changing commercial and investment banking industries. A year in New York in the mid-1970s, five years in New York, Montreal, and Toronto in the late 1970s and early 1980s, and nearly a year in Toronto again in the mid-1980s almost qualify as a career, these days anyway.

Thanks to an International Affairs Fellowship from the Council on Foreign Relations and a leave from the University of Toronto on the cusp of a new decade, I had the chance to develop that career one step further during a year on the staff of the International Monetary Fund. Although I thought about staying, the siren song of the academy called me back. If this book does not help old friends understand exactly why I made apparently irrational decisions to leave more lucrative positions in what they often call "the real world," it will at least give them a glimpse into what I have been doing since then.

During my time at the IMF and since then, I got to know Joseph Gold and Jacques Polak. This book began to take its shape in the course of our many conversations. Like so many other scholars they have helped over their long and incredibly fruitful lives, I am in their debt. For the insights of other conversations and a few formal interviews, I record my gratitude as well to Mark Allen, the late Edward Bernstein, James Boughton, Ralph Bryant, Robert Bryce, Ian Clark, William Dale, Jacques de Larosière, André de Lattre, Margaret Garritsen de Vries, Wendy Dobson, Bernard Drabble, Wolfgang Duchatczek, Dieter Eckert, Richard Erb, David Finch, Martin Gilman, Manuel Guitián, Toyoo Gyohten, Robert Holzmann, Peter Kenen, Pen Kent, Marcel Massé, Christopher McMahon, Jeremy Morse, Shigeo Nakao, Yuichiro Nagatomi, Yoshio Okubo, Sylvia Ostry, Eckard Pieske, Lionel Price, Louis Rasminsky, Robert Raymond, Klaus Regling, Jürgen Reitmaier, Klaus Riechel, Wolfgang Rieke, Robert Russell, Eisuke Sakakibara, Heinrich Schneider, Aurel Schubert, Robert Solomon, Susan Strange, Andre Szász, Geza Tatrallyay, Maxwell Watson, John Williamson, Georg Winckler, H. Johannes Witteveen, and Edwin Yeo.

Thanks also to Ursula-Maria Ruser and Alfred Guindi of the League of Nations Archives in Geneva, Switzerland, and to Henry Gillett, archivist of the Bank of England. I was assisted as well by various staff members of the national archives of Canada and of the United States. Although I had access to confidential materials at the Fund, I did not need them for present purposes. I also attended occasional meetings of the Fund's Executive Board, but again relied on no privileged information learned there. (The archives of the Fund have recently been opened under a thirty-year rule, subject to exceptions for certain sensitive matters.)

This book might never have seen the light of day without the sustained interest and gentle prodding of Roger Haydon of Cornell University Press, the best editor in the field. For constructive comments on parts of the manuscript, I am grateful to Philip Cerny, Stephen Gill, Eric Helleiner, C. Randall Henning, Harold James, Evert Lindquist, Stephen Newman, and Kenneth Rogoff. I am even more deeply indebted to David Andrews, Miles Kahler, Michael

Webb, and especially Benjamin Cohen for close readings of the entire draft. David McIver, Linda White, Michelle Cloutier, and Jo-Anne Gestrin provided much-appreciated research assistance. All of the individuals named are responsible for any strengths of this book, but none is responsible for its weaknesses. Generous financial support came from the Social Sciences and Humanities Research Council of Canada, the Council on Foreign Relations, and the Department of Political Science of the University of Toronto. The Institute of Advanced Studies in Vienna kindly provided office facilities during two lengthy stays, and the Brookings Institution did the same during one sojourn in Washington.

I have lectured and written on the themes of this book for several years now. Jochen Lorentzen, Roger Morgan, Andreas Schedler, Janice Gross Stein, Richard Stubbs, and Geoffrey Underhill helped me shape those themes into related essays. The following essays contain substantial portions of text developed further herein, and I thank the publishers for their support: "The League of Nations and the Foreshadowing of the International Monetary Fund," *Essays in International Finance,* no. 201 (December 1996), Copyright © 1996, adapted and reproduced by permission of the International Finance Section of Princeton University; "Capital Mobility, State Autonomy, and Political Legitimacy," *Journal of International Affairs* 48, no. 2 (1995): 369–88, adapted and reproduced by permission of the *Journal* and the Trustees of Columbia University in the City of New York; and "The Political Foundations of Multilateral Economic Surveillance," *International Journal* 47, no. 2 (1992): 293–327, adapted and reproduced by permission of the Canadian Institute of International Affairs.

When we moved to Washington, my wife was willing to bundle up a toddler, a newborn infant, and her own not-yet-finished doctoral dissertation. That brave decision and this book are inextricably linked. Despite the many challenges that followed Caryl's decision, she is now a professor herself, and Tessa and Reid are experienced world travelers. They know how much I owe them.

LOUIS W. PAULY

Toronto, Canada

Who Elected the Bankers?

CHAPTER I

Global Markets and National Politics

A PROFOUND TRANSFORMATION IS UNDER WAY IN THE
world economy. No consensus exists yet, either in the market-
place or in the academy, about its nature or its ultimate implications.
But many now feel the changes involved, and they express that feeling in one word: "globalization."

Nowhere have we heard the mantra of change repeated more
often than on Wall Street, in the City of London, and in other world
financial centers. Pressed for examples of what the term means, the
mind now turns automatically to the image of more integrated financial markets, through which international capital flows ever more
fluidly. The image conjures up feelings of liberation and boundless
possibilities in some privileged quarters, a troubling sense of foreboding in most others.

A currency trader in Asia brings down a venerable merchant
bank in Britain. The failure of a bank incorporated in Luxembourg
rocks distant firms whose managers are only dimly aware of their
connection to it. Political leaders at summit meetings of the world's
richest countries proclaim themselves to be bound by the constraints
of global markets. New finance ministers from around the world

make the seemingly obligatory pilgrimage to New York as they start their terms in office. The homeless are told that their indebted governments are unable to help them.

Many people now fear "global" finance, and their fear is not irrational. It is rooted in a dilemma of political legitimacy that deepens with each new step toward markets that are truly integrated across national political borders. That dilemma lies at the center of this book.

The Conflicting Logics of Markets and Politics

By any standard, the scale and speed of international financial flows today is striking, so striking that many observers now characterize ours as a new era in the economic history of the world. In fact, very high levels of capital mobility helped define the global order before 1914. But war and depression across much of the twentieth century effectively destroyed it. The current deepening integration of financial markets is an attempt to restore at least part of that earlier order.

In comparison with the terrible decades at the center of the twentieth century, or even with the decades of the recently ended Cold War, this new world of expanded mobility for international capital obviously has its attractions. But the sense of unease now commonly conjured up by the image of emerging global capital markets is palpable, especially in societies that call themselves democratic. It manifests a perfectly reasonable fear: that the evolution of such markets means, in effect, that the power to make substantive decisions affecting our own material prospects and the prospects of our children is currently shifting out of our control.

The chief negotiators of the 1944 Bretton Woods agreement, which established the parameters of the postwar international monetary system and created the International Monetary Fund and the World Bank, confronted this dilemma directly. They could see no way around the fact that states, if they valued economic stability as much as they valued their political independence, would have to maintain the capacity to deploy capital controls.[1]

Half a century later, states remain capable of influencing the movement of capital across their borders, but the possibility of actually controlling such movements at acceptable political cost is very substantially reduced. Formal controls, where they continue to exist, are typically seen as transitional in nature or, more commonly, as a sign of serious economic and political weakness. International financial integration is the order of the day, especially among advanced industrial democracies. Although capital remains more mobile within national economies than between them, something like global capital markets appear on the horizon. Advanced industrial states did the most actually to promote such a development during the past few decades, so it is ironic that even they now confront a more profound version of the dilemma their negotiators anticipated in 1944.

In Canada, for example, many citizens are now beginning to sense the implications of ever more deeply integrated North American financial markets. Even as they themselves advance that process through their own decisions about savings and investments, they are asking themselves whether the ultimate consequence of those decisions must be more complete integration with the United States. Economists remind them that other choices are possible; Canadians just have to be willing to bear the costs. Those who bother to listen seem aware that the politics involved are not simple.

With a greater sense of urgency, Europeans find themselves confronting similar questions as financial linkages deepen across formerly distinct national economies. By the latter 1990s, it was the contentious politics of monetary union which set the terms of debate on the future of the great experiment in community-building begun after the conflagration of World War II. German Chancellor Helmut Kohl was warning that failure threatened to awaken sleeping demons even as opponents of a broad and deep European monetary union grew more strident. At the same time, internal debates on political reform in Japan commonly began with the assertion that mounting financial challenges—"shocks," in the local parlance— required high degrees of adaptability in long-standing domestic arrangements. Throughout the 1990s even Americans, whose social history suggests a remarkable willingness to embrace change, were asking themselves whether they were losing control over basic economic forces that affected their lives.[2] A long-standing sense of immunity to international financial pressures seemed to be eroding.

Outside the advanced industrial world, any sense of immunity has long since been replaced by the knowledge of vulnerability. In the mid-1990s, Mexico provided the most conspicuous example of how the daily lives of average citizens can be utterly disrupted when national policies fall out of line with the expectations of international financiers. The Mexican experience is hardly unique in the developing world.

On the surface, the domestic challenges presented by the image or reality of external financial constraints reflect the straightforward consequences of national debts and deficits. Much popular commentary focuses on this seemingly self-evident observation. But something deeper is also at work. Increasingly integrated private capital markets are no accident. The policies of national governments crafted and shaped them. But many national governments now are ill-equipped to deal with their ultimately political implications.

One set of political implications is linked to the challenge of simultaneously enhancing market efficiency and preventing market failure when regulatory power becomes more decentralized. Another involves social demands for protection from the tender mercies of efficient markets. Both lie behind the concerns of citizens when they confront the image or the reality of global financial integration.

Those concerns are not atavistic. Schooling in the technical intricacies of high finance will not calm them. They are not holdovers from a more primitive time when people thought that national economic development was, or should be, controlled by their own states. They are instead the perfectly understandable manifestations of a deepening paradox.

Political economists have recognized the paradox ever since they began to write about the underpinnings of international interdependence.[3] Political theorists have noted it ever since they began debating the content and meaning of the oxymoron "democratic capitalism." In its simplest terms, it is this: the logic of markets is borderless, but the logic of politics remains bounded.

The main architects of the emergent global economy—the governments of advanced industrial democracies and their citizens—want the best of both worlds. They want the fruits that financial openness appears to promise, and they also want real influence over the shape of the tree. Their desires are in tension and cannot be fully satisfied. But some governments and some citizens can come close.

International Institutions and Deep Integration

Imagine a spectrum of world political orders that extends from the purely autonomous management of discrete national economies at one end to the joint management of fully integrated economies at the other end.[4] The institution at the heart of the former order would be the classical sovereign state, uncontested, isolated, and uncooperative. At the other end would be a supranational governing institution, perhaps analogous to a federal state. Somewhere near the midpoint of the spectrum would lie a weakly institutionalized order wherein interdependent but still sovereign states, motivated either by the desire to avoid common evils or by the need to secure common goods, voluntarily coordinated their policies. Facilitating deeper collaborative work would be a set of agreed rules and behavioral norms, a neutral institutional forum for continuous negotiations on mutual policy adjustments, and a dedicated secretariat to refine and monitor those rules and to support those negotiations.[5]

Now imagine a spectrum of world economic orders, ranging from separated national markets to truly global markets. Around the midpoint we would find increasingly integrated national markets. Contemporary capital markets exemplify such a midpoint. As we shall see, however, they seem to have moved in recent years from the less integrated side of the spectrum to the more integrated.

The deepening tension between the trajectory of national politics and the trajectory of international finance may be imagined in terms of these two spectrums. Core aspects of the contemporary economic order and its political analog may still be located near the midpoints of the respective spectrums, but they appear to be moving in opposite directions. Financial integration is on the rise, whereas political integration, with the important exception of western Europe, is not a self-evident trend.

One means actually to resolve the various political tensions attending the emergence of truly global capital markets lies at one extreme end of the political spectrum. At that point are effective instruments of global governance. Another means of resolving those tensions is to move back along the economic spectrum toward dis-integrated markets. Neither option is attractive. The first conjures images of tyranny, the second calls forth the specter of world depression.

There are many points imaginable between the two extremes, albeit not for resolving the ever-greater political tensions associated with economic and financial integration but for coping with them. In the decades before World War I, for example, certain states chose a point that we now label "the gold standard" in our history books. In practice, those states gave pride of place to the logic of markets at a time when the political claims of ordinary citizens were much less expansive than they are today. In retrospect, both the international anchor provided by the gold standard and the absence of what we call today the welfare state or the entitlement state seemed necessary conditions for global capital markets to flourish; and indeed, flourish they did. The speed of cross-border capital movements may have been limited by our contemporary standards, but the scale of global finance in those days was not a mere abstraction. It was embodied in the cross-national relationships among the Morgans and the Warburgs, the Wallenbergs and the Schiffs, the Cassels, the Harrimans, and the Rockefellers. For them, 1914 marked the end of an era.

By the end of the twentieth century, advanced industrial democracies had collectively chosen another point on the economic and political spectrums. Their choice was significantly shaped by entrenched societal demands for economic security.[6] On the one hand, they allowed their national markets to become more deeply integrated. On the other hand, they created a set of international and regional political institutions. In terms of raw power, most of those institutions, both individually and collectively, are relatively weak. That weakness belies their true importance.

International economic and financial institutions serve a number of purposes. The integration of capital markets implicates two of them. If we think of those markets as a building, international institutions would comprise two elements in its structure. The first is the plumbing, the second the foundation.

Most relevant political studies focus on the plumbing underneath international capital markets, and the literature grows very rapidly whenever a pipe bursts. Bank failures, debt crises, catastrophic spillovers of trouble from one financial market to another—all have captured the attention of policymakers as well as policy analysts. So too have institutional responses, from the expansion of emergency lending facilities through specific organizations to the negotiation of supervisory understandings.[7] In the main, this is the realm of central banks and the regulators of banking and securities markets. Although most of these actors were created by states, many of them now enjoy a significant degree of formal independence from governmental executives, legislatures, and courts.[8]

Less well known are the invisible political foundations of our international financial building. The chief architects remain states, and specific governments speak for them, mainly through their finance ministries and chief executives but also through their legislatures. Their principal drafting tools are monetary and fiscal policies.[9] Through such macroeconomic policies, more precisely through the interaction of those policies under conditions of interdependence, states stabilize or destabilize the markets that they have collectively established and nurtured.

International institutions arise in just such a context, and their task is to facilitate stabilization. That, in any event, is what the textbooks tell us when they set out the agenda of macroeconomic policy coordination and international monetary collaboration. And although we will explore this claim more fully below, this is what finance ministers, their deputies, and their staffs say they are pursuing when they regularly consult with one another in the International Monetary Fund (the IMF or Fund) and various other organizational forums, from the Group of Seven to the Organization for Economic Cooperation and Development (OECD). Skeptics commonly claim that markets basically run themselves, achieve their own natural equilibria, and ultimately bind their erstwhile architects. International organizations, they assert, are epiphenomenal. At best, they promote the provision of information to those markets; at worst, they impede market efficiency. Both the plumbing and the foundations of contemporary international capital markets are now effectively privatized, argue the skeptics. Morgan, Warburg, and their colleagues have been resurrected, albeit as faceless private corporations bearing names such as Citibank, Deutsche Bank, and Nomura Securities. International financial institutions like the IMF speak for them. This book finds such a view problematic.

The IMF and its foreshadowing are at the center of this book, but I do not claim to provide a comprehensive organizational analysis. The reason that the evolution of the Fund is of interest here is because it sheds light on the actual political foundations of the capital markets now so prominent a feature of the international economy. More important than global-market enthusiasts claim and less powerful than opponents of globalization believe, the IMF reflects a long and continuing struggle to design the political architecture for global capital markets. The United States and other advanced industrial democracies have led the effort in the contemporary era, but their organizational agenda was presaged much earlier in the twentieth century when Great Britain played the leading role.

The IMF is today emblematic of the many organizations and forums that now comprise the machinery of a relatively weak international regime for economic policy coordination and a fragile but strengthening regime for financial crisis management. It has the most comprehensive membership, for nearly all states in the world are members. It also has the clearest legal mandate, the largest professional staff, and significant financial resources under its own day-to-day control. It nevertheless remains an intergovernmental institution, and its basic policies and functions mirror the intentions of its members, especially its leading members.

Under the terms of its principal mandate, first implied in a multi-lateral treaty on exchange rate arrangements negotiated in 1944 and made explicit some thirty years later when that treaty was amended, the Fund is charged with providing "firm surveillance" over the international monetary system.[10] We will explore the meaning of that phrase more fully below.[11] At the outset, however, it is important to emphasize that this defining role and its international legal grounding now underpin all of the Fund's activities, from providing balance of payments and emergency financing to members in need to advising them on technical matters. Over time, that role necessarily led to IMF engagement with all issues touching on the interaction of the macroeconomic polices of its member-states, policies that, once again, are the very foundations for integrating capital markets.

The development of the Fund's principal role thus provides a unique window on international capital markets. The story holds rich insights into the ways in which states have collectively attempted to cope with the rising tension between the logic of global markets and the logic of national politics. Indeed, if borderless markets and bounded politics are the tectonic plates of an emergent world order, the edifice of the IMF itself is built on the main fault line.

This book introduces analogs and competitors to the Fund, but at its empirical core it focuses on the historical emergence of the Fund's principal mandate. On its face, the continuing weakness of that mandate, especially when it comes to promoting system-stabilizing adjustments in the economic policies of leading states, poses a puzzle. If stable and truly global markets do require stronger political foundations, and if states are truly committed to building such markets, that mandate should be strengthening. Even if it is not located inside the Fund, it would seem to be required somewhere, especially at a time when no single state can ensure systemic stability on its own.[12] Conversely, if such foundations are not required in a world of increasingly privatized finance, the loose regime that the Fund embodies should disappear. The central weakness *and* the stubborn endurance of that regime in a new era of global finance need to be explained.

Although now largely forgotten, the effort to restore integrated capital markets to the very center of the world economy dates back to the days of the League of Nations, and more specifically to the evolving mandate of the Economic and Financial Organization, which grew up inside the League. Then, as well as now, that effort implied the establishment of an international organizational base. In this book, I trace the roots of the Fund's principal mandate back to the League.

The standard economic analysis of global financial integration emphasizes the trade-offs that exist for states between capital mobility, exchange rate stability, and monetary autonomy. International legal analysis of the same phenomenon stresses the ancient choice states have faced between a world of rules and a world of discretion. Such approaches provide a necessary starting point, and both are introduced in the following chapters. But the story of the IMF and its foreshadowing in the League ultimately needs to be understood in a more focused political context.

Two sorts of political controversies now regularly bring the IMF to the attention of nonspecialist audiences. When it hits the headlines, the Fund is usually depicted as a convenient tool by which industrial countries can influence developing countries or countries in transition from socialism. In this context, it is often seen as attempting to strong-arm countries into conformity with dominant behavioral norms. It is viewed, in short, as a weapon wielded by leading states to open and develop new markets.

The other controversy frequently calling attention to the Fund and its central role is more subtle. It is the sort of attention we pay to an empty chair in a crowded meeting room. When its rich member-states design their own economic policies, policies that cannot help but affect the world economy more generally, the Fund, ostensibly evenhanded in its analysis and advocacy, is often depicted as irrelevant.

There is plenty of evidence to support criticisms of the IMF and its leading member-states from both points of view. Much of the evidence is discussed in this book. But I develop another theme as I trace the origins of the Fund's principal role and introduce its contemporary analogs. Beneath the arcane economic rites and Delphic pronouncements of the Fund lies an important legal obligation.

Unlike their counterparts in the League, the member-states of the Fund formally hold themselves accountable to one another for the external implications of their own internal decisions on economic policy. Such an obligation, to be sure, is modest. But in view of the jealousy with which states have traditionally guarded their autonomy, it is a significant departure. Its acceptance represents a response, imperfect though it may be, to one of the most profound conundrums of politics under conditions of intensifying financial integration. It reflects, in short, the increasingly difficult search for political legitimacy within states themselves at a time when the ideology of globalism is resurgent. Beyond its more obvious purposes, the Fund, as well as many of its analogs, are political instruments for coping with a fundamental contradiction which that ideology cannot overcome.

One does not have to be an economist or a political scientist to recognize the basic conflict between international economics and national politics. The simple fact is that even people who are happy to let cosmopolitan norms guide their material lives are typically unwilling to submit to supranational political authorities. We live in an age when markets are essentially political creations, but no polity is capable of creating a seamless global market. As recent European history attests, even the establishment of functioning regional polities to ground robust regional markets is enormously difficult and intrinsically ambiguous. And even the casual observer will have noted the ironic spread of demands for national political autonomy at a time when international economic integration is apparently intensifying.

The core problem is an old one. The power to determine, in Harold Lasswell's famous phrase, "who gets what, when, and how" may be wielded directly or indirectly. In the modern era, states are the principal wielders of power, although they have never exercised a monopoly on it.[13] In our day, a long history of social experimentation has culminated in paramountcy for one particular indirect instrumentality of state power—the instrumentality of legal markets. The word "legal" is important, for it sums up a significant tradition of thought of direct relevance to the empirical exploration of this book.

Political Legitimacy and Global Markets

Historical and sociological research on the forces behind the simultaneous development of the market economy and the modern state is currently flourishing.[14] A rough consensus exists on one point. Except in certain radical ideological fraternities often mistakenly labeled "conservative," it is widely acknowledged that advanced industrial capitalism involves an intimate union between the state and the market.

In practice, the authority of the state and the deference of mass populations to basic norms of market behavior are now inextricably linked. The Industrial Revolution strengthened those links, and the vast political and social transformations wrought by the Great Depression and its military aftermath redoubled them. Just as the authority of the state today undergirds the market, so too the performance of the market now bears significantly on the authority of the state. Ever since Max Weber sketched the outlines for a systematic theory of political legitimacy, students of politics have used it to differentiate such authority from raw power.[15] At base, the theory emphasizes a psychological relationship.

Legitimacy derives from the extent to which a claimed right to exercise power is matched by the perception of an obligation to comply.[16] This is the essence of what the ancient Romans called the rule of law, and scholars now quite commonly deploy it at three levels of political analysis. At the most general level, we apply the concept to entire world orders or to systems of governance that transcend national borders. At the most specific level, we speak of the legitimacy of a particular government which, once it loses the confidence of its constituents, must or should be replaced. At an intermediate level between world orders and individual governments, we use the concept to assess the basic strength or weakness of the generic form of political organization characteristic of the modern age, the state.[17] Although it touches on the issue of political legitimacy at all three levels of analysis at various points in its narrative, this book focuses on the last usage. As the empirical chapters will suggest, the very idea of markets beyond the state directly threatens the legitimacy of the state itself in the modern era. International institutions such as the IMF need to be understood in just such a context.

There has, in fact, never been a single answer to the problem of legitimacy for all states and at all times. Despite the textbook story to the effect that "divine right" once was sufficient to entrance the builders of states and cow their subject populations, establishing and maintaining the legitimacy of state power has always been difficult. The main reason is that even before states replaced their historical competitors, the notion that political authority derived from the willing acquiescence of more or less defined populations was well understood. The history of this idea is fascinating, but a full survey would take us too far from our main theme.[18]

Suffice it to note that various states used various devices to secure the support, or at least the acquiescence, of their populations at the dawn of the industrial era. The United States, for example, combined the liberal principles enshrined in its Declaration of Independence with a written constitution, the institutions of representative government, and a civic religion of inclusive nationalism. In deliberate contrast to "life, liberty, and the pursuit of happiness," the fathers of the Canadian confederation gave primacy to the ideals of peace, order, and good government and a dualistic nationalism mediated by the institutions of a hybrid form of British parliamentarianism. Other states staked their claims to legitimacy on a more explicit and exclusive articulation of the national principle.

To be sure, there was an economic dimension to all of these claims. At a minimum, the state became the definer of the basic property rights upon which growing national markets depended. At a maximum, it replaced those markets. Most, however, operated on the middle ground. Private markets were means to ends, and even where they came to resemble ends in themselves, the state was increasingly called upon to cushion their more politically charged consequences. Bismarck, after all, is correctly viewed as the father of the welfare state. By the mid-twentieth century, the authority of the state and the performance of the *national* economy had become intimately linked, especially in advanced industrial democracies.

With the rise of the modern welfare state in the aftermath of world depression and world war, state power and the socially constructive performance of markets fused in a new way.[19] The "community of interests" required to sustain the political authority of the state could no longer be fostered by the liberal economic system bequeathed by the Industrial Revolution, a system some critics labeled "laissez-faire" and others called imperialist. Out of the cauldron of World War II came a new compromise, a compromise to which an expanding group of states acceded in subsequent decades. The compromise joined the ideal of liberal international markets with the practical reality of national economic regulation. The historic compromise was never neat, unambiguous, or unquestioned. But everyone knew it existed, not least, as we shall see in the next chapter, people in the capital markets.

After the Cold War ended, it seemed to many observers that this compromise, by now enshrined in the myriad structures of the modern welfare state, was quickly unraveling. Capitalist imperatives in an era of global markets and democratic necessity in a world of distinct nation-states appeared to be in fundamental conflict, a conflict manifested in strident debates over public finances, widening income disparities, and anxieties concerning social and cultural homogenization. The central idea suggested by such debates, that these developments could call into question the legitimacy of the modern state itself, has had a long gestation.

Over two centuries ago, Adam Smith showed how liberal, market-based economies work through incentives that are necessarily distributed in an inequitable manner. In the contemporary period, the state, in principle, oversees the distribution of those incentives either directly by fiat or indirectly through markets. In either case, its ability to do so depends upon its authority, which, once again, may be conceived of as power that has somehow been legitimated. When it acts directly, say through redistributive fiscal policies, as well as when it acts indirectly, say by regulating or supervising financial markets, it exercises that authority. But such actions pose an acute dilemma when authority derives from the consent of the governed, all of whom must in some sense see themselves as politically equal.

Capitalist democracies face a multidimensional challenge if they are to maintain a necessary sense of legitimacy among their citizens. Out of a confluence of leading traditions of thought on that challenge flows the basic idea that two sets of priorities—a growing economy and responsible government—are today required for a critical mass of citizens to accept the authority of their state.

As one political theorist phrases it, that sense of legitimacy now involves "first, the ability of each set of priorities to retain the reflective allegiance of most citizens and, second, the continued ability of each priority to exist in harmony with the other."[20] Stable growth, with its fruits shared widely, is conducive to harmony. Unstable growth, a concentration of wealth, and an unresponsive government, conversely, cannot help but work in the opposite direction.

But how much growth is enough, and how much inequality can be tolerated before the communal fabric cloaking the exercise of state power begins to fray? No one can say, and the answer appears to vary for different societies. In the mid-1990s, following two decades of very low economic growth for the average citizen in most industrial democracies and of actual decline in poorer countries, much popular commentary suggested that the limits of tolerance were uncomfortably close. At the same time, a mounting body of scholarly research contended that the syndrome of economic activities encompassed by the term "globalization" worked to increase inequalities both inside distinct societies and across them.[21] Common sense suggested that it did so by rewarding the mobile and penalizing the immobile.[22]

Throughout the postwar period, the promise of reliable economic growth provided democratic capitalist states with their primary means not for solving the long-standing dilemma resulting from the combination of democracy and capitalism, but for keeping it within acceptable limits. The task is today vastly compounded as states have sought that growth ever more assertively though external economic expansion. Not just trade but also international investment, international production, and international finance now define the leading edges of our modern economies. The task of shielding domestic societies becomes more complex, and the complexity deepens when external expansion fails to bring reliable or equitable returns.

More concretely, citizens in democratic societies continue to hold the government of their own state—alone—responsible for widening economic prosperity.[23] If that government cannot deliver prosperity, it may be replaced. If, however, those same citizens ever perceive effective governing authority to have somehow dissipated into a supranational ether, they would find themselves up against the legitimacy crisis that theorists have been speculating about for years. Attempting to respond to the rising anxieties of its citizens, a government might make desperate moves to wrest control back, only to find that economic catastrophe has unmasked the true nature of the crisis. The state itself has become obsolete.

This obviously paints the picture in overly bright colors. Or does it? Why is there so much talk on the left of "transnational" coalitions that might mobilize to counter the rising influence of global corporations and global financiers?[24] Why is there so much talk on the right about decentralizing government and empowering local communities? And why, in country after country, is there now such a turning away even among centrists from the prospect of "politics as usual"?

A handful of states are still of sufficient size and dynamism to affect the terms of economic integration more than that process affects them. For such states the legitimacy problem is often obscured. The United States, Germany, and Japan come to mind, and the following chapters will have much to say about the distinctions that survive between them and most others. Outside leading states, however, the political problem associated with economic integration is becoming much clearer.

A truly global economy is in many ways still a liberal dream. In most markets the ultimate economic test of globalism—the prevalence of one price (adjusted for transport costs) across geographically separated markets—is not yet being passed. In none are the more demanding tests of institutional analysis met; in history, single markets have depended, for example, upon clearly established property rights, common understandings of appropriate behavior, and reliable dispute-settlement procedures. But the institutional threads of globalism are becoming visible, particularly in financial markets, and evidence of an emergent legitimacy problem is all around us.

It is palpable in right-wing political platforms, even in the United States, Germany, and Japan. It complicates struggles on the left to articulate clear responses to contemporary economic challenges. It can be heard in the alarm bells that ring in finance ministries and central banks around the world when exchange rates come under attack. Like a shadow, it lurks in the background when private credit rating agencies mark down the value of a government's debt.[25] It lies in the corners of boardrooms when globe-spanning corporations design their "hedging" strategies. It also helps explain both the endurance and the weakness of international institutions such as the IMF.

The Plan and Argument of the Book

The conflict between global economic imperatives and national political responsibilities has shaped a weakly institutionalized regime for macroeconomic policy coordination and crisis management, a regime that provides the political architecture for international capital markets. The International Monetary Fund and its central mandate comprise key pieces of that architecture. The next chapter covers the basic economic and financial concepts needed to understand the Fund's mandate, its origins, its limitations, and its analogs. The chapters that follow trace its historical development across the turbulent twentieth century. Unlike most accounts, they depict the main work of the Fund as foreshadowed not in the famous negotiations that took place at Bretton Woods, but in the underresearched experience of the League of Nations.

The narrative of these empirical chapters may be read as four case studies or as two sets of comparisons. History may be a seamless web, but the character of the organizational mandate examined across the cases varies in fairly systematic ways. The 1920s precursor to the IMF and its analogs was relatively more robust than the one that emerged in the 1930s. The post-1970s mandate of the IMF and its analogs was more robust than its 1950s antecedent. The central mandates of both organizations, implicitly in the case of the League and explicitly in the case of the IMF, involved the oversight of national policies, most directly under conditions of financial crisis, and systemic oversight, mainly with a view to overall economic stability. That role required both organizations to promote convergent policies among weaker states, and they recorded some successes. It also required politically difficult policy coordination among leading states, however, and in this context both organizations found themselves on the margins. To measure the precise degree of marginalization at any particular time is to assess the durability of the political architecture of international capital markets.

The concluding chapter summarizes a political explanation for the evolving mandates of the Economic and Financial Organization of the League and of the IMF, an explanation linked to a long, quixotic struggle to restore global capital markets without fundamentally undermining the legitimacy of the state. In an interdependent system characterized more by hierarchy than by anarchy, that is, by major differences in financial power between leading states and all others, that explanation contrasts the motive force arising from the fear of common economic evils with that arising from the desire for common economic goods.[26] When political legitimacy still attaches most deeply to the state, the fear of common economic evils can call forth reliable multilateral collaboration, for it promises to preserve the integrity of the state. The desire for common economic goods, however, is rarely sufficient on its own to provide a foundation for solidly institutionalizing that collaboration, for it threatens over time to undermine the integrity of the state. Crisis management to avoid mutual losses is therefore much easier than policy coordination to harness mutual gains. The pristine legal ideal of "sovereignty" is not the goal. Even under conditions of deepening economic interdependence which they themselves promote, states are still driven by the need to preserve their fundamental political legitimacy. International institutions like the one at the center of this book are born in such an environment.

When states delegate effective authority to actors in private markets, both the act of delegation and the future performance of those actors have implications for their own continued legitimacy. Organizations like the IMF would not have evolved as they did if the expansion of international capital markets had not raised significant legitimacy issues for states, even for the leading states that shaped core organizational mandates. Such a contention is far from obvious, particularly at a time when public debate tends to emphasize the growing irrelevance of international organizations to the deepest interests of those states.

The story of the IMF, and of the foreshadowing and development of its core mandate, is the story of states advancing the cause of deeper economic and financial integration. Beneath the surface, however, it is about states, especially leading states, attempting to buffer themselves from the threat of delegitimation posed by that process. For in the end, they want to approach global markets without ever actually attaining them.

CHAPTER 2

The Political Economy of International Capital Mobility

IN THE 1990S, FROM POLITICAL CAMPAIGNS TO THE PAGES OF learned journals, debates over the meaning, advisability, and practice of multilateral economic management have come to the fore. The United Nations, the World Bank, the World Trade Organization, the International Monetary Fund—all found themselves under attack. Nowhere were those debates sharper than in the United States. There was a good deal of irony in this, for Washington had promoted the central idea behind those institutions in the first place.

To a new generation of "America Firsters," multilateralism had come to represent an ideological challenge as profound as the earlier challenges of communism and socialism. In the run-up to the 1996 presidential election, even moderate Republicans such as Robert Dole referred to multilateralism as a "myth" that "we don't need anymore."[1] His immoderate opponent for the party's nomination, Patrick Buchanan, equated multilateralism with "world government." "I know that those folks in Tokyo, New York, Paris, Bonn, Brussels, they love this idea of world government," Buchanan stated in a speech to the legislature of New Hampshire, "but if I am elected

President of the United States, the minute I raise my hand to take that oath of office that new world order comes crashing down."[2]

To students of contemporary American foreign policy, on the other hand, multilateralism was the very essence of an international economic system crafted by the United States in its own image.[3] On this view, any "crashing down" would be as much a domestic convulsion as a foreign one.

The ties of international economic and financial interdependence have never been as taut for the United States as for most other industrial countries, but they are now nearly as evident to the farmer in Peoria and the entrepreneur in St. Louis as they are to the securities trader in New York and the air traffic controller in Chicago. Even so, those ties obviously remain invisible to many.

The impulses toward and away from the particular multilateral institution at the center of this book reflect a fascinating interplay between politics and economics during a tumultuous century. In order to understand the fundamental contest over legitimacy at the core of that politics, we need to start with the economics.

The Problem of Adjustment in Open Economies

Pretend, for a moment, that the negative consequences of economic interdependence—"globalization," as many now call it—could all be quantified. Economists would term them "adjustment costs." That the benefits of economic specialization and international exchange outweigh such costs is given, otherwise the exchange would not occur. But it is the uneven distribution of those benefits and costs which makes the politics of interdependence so interesting and so precarious.

Political scientists commonly ask how adjustment costs *are* actually distributed, both across societies and within them. Economists commonly, and usually implicitly, ask how they *should* be distributed. Reality is complex, but in principle the options are few. From the point of view of states, the central actors in the international system, five are feasible in a world where market mechanisms provide the deepest economic linkages among them.

First, states can unilaterally decide simply to accept whatever distribution "naturally" occurs through the interaction of markets. Second, states can unilaterally decide to attempt to shift some of those costs, through markets, onto other states and their societies. Third, distribution issues can be negotiated with other states on a bilateral basis. Fourth, regional political institutions can be built to mediate the process of adjustment and to channel or offset grievances in a constructive manner. Finally, more broadly based multilateral institutions can be designed to promote a politically more acceptable distribution of adjustment costs on the basis of the rules that govern markets.[4]

Examples of the first four options abound in modern economic history. We shall examine below an unsuccessful experiment along the lines of the fifth option, which occurred before World War II. After the war, when the United States moved to remake the world in the image of Franklin Roosevelt's New Deal, the experiment was revived.[5] Broadly based multilateral institutions like the United Nations, the World Bank, and the International Monetary Fund reflected that movement.

The commitment of the United States and its principal allies to the postwar experiment in multilateralism, never of overwhelming strength, was soon tested as they pursued a variety of more limited and more discretionary adjustment strategies. Throughout the postwar period, in fact, no clear pattern emerged. Multilateral advances in trade policy, for example, were matched by a resurgence of regional arrangements, bilateral bargaining, and unilateral initiatives and by the emergence of international institutions with limited memberships. Still, the quest for an encompassing multilateral order was never abandoned. Even as they stretched the rules of the early postwar order to the breaking point, leading states would always pull back from the point of no return.

There is a price to pay as national economies adjust to market openness, and the choice of particular institutional mechanisms for distributing the costs reflects at base the most fundamental of political decisions: the choice between rules and discretion, between law and arbitrary power.[6] In a world where leading states remain capable of unilateral policy changes, and where they continue to rely on bilateral, regional, or exclusive bargaining arrangements, it is obviously difficult in the late twentieth century to argue that rule-based and inclusive multilateralism was an inevitable path to the future. In the real world, however, the most basic trade-offs have rarely been unambiguous. The point is well illustrated in the arena of money and finance.

Whatever particular path of international adjustment is actually chosen, monetary and financial openness entails an intrinsic linkage between the internal balances of national economies and their external balances. Quantity and price measures of internal performance typically encompass the output of goods and services, savings and investment, productivity, employment, wages, money supplies, interest rates, and inflation rates. Measures of external performance focus on the balance between outward and inward flows of payments for goods and services bought and sold (the current account of the balance of payments), the balance between inward and outward flows of investment (the capital account), and the exchange rate.

When economies are open and impersonal markets are allowed to work as broadly as possible, all of these measures affect one another. When national financial markets are linked and central banks do not attempt to offset capital inflows or outflows, interest rates and exchange rates necessarily interact. This situation implies certain policy trade-offs. An elegant model, first developed by two IMF economists in the early 1960s, sketches out the most important.[7]

The Mundell-Fleming model essentially showed that governments and central banks overseeing open economies cannot simultaneously maintain the independence of their internal monetary policies, stabilize their exchange rates, and permit unrestricted inward and outward capital movements.[8] As interest rates, inflation rates, and exchange rates influence one another under conditions of openness, over time only two of these policy goals at most can be achieved.[9] If priority is given to open capital markets and stable exchange rates, domestic interest rates will reflect external developments. When the autonomy of national monetary policy and exchange-rate stability are prized, capital movements must be limited. Finally, if capital mobility and monetary autonomy are preferred, exchange rates must be allowed to adjust.

When fiscal policy—the taxing and spending activities of governments—is brought into the Mundell-Fleming framework, the standard economic analysis is also straightforward. When exchange rates are flexible and capital is perfectly mobile, changes in monetary policy become the only effective tool for influencing national economic performance; changes in fiscal policy cease to have any effect. Alternatively, when exchange rates are fixed or capital movements are controlled, fiscal policy becomes effective and monetary policy ineffective. Such trade-offs are forced by systematic and predictable changes in spending, saving, and investing behavior.

In sum: the more open economies become to inward and outward capital flows, the more difficult it is for governments to maintain stable exchange rates and monetary policies fully sensitive to national priorities. If unilateral monetary actions are nevertheless taken, say money supplies are constricted to dampen inflation, exchange rates will immediately come under pressure. If governments wish their fiscal policies to retain their capacity to reinforce the monetary policy line, they will have to find ways to dissipate that pressure. In practice, this means that if they are committed to exchange-rate stability, they will have to find ways to modify or impede the flow of capital.

Refinements and modifications of this model have filled academic journals and textbooks over the past thirty years, but the model's central message continues to ground the study of open-economy macroeconomics.[10] The space for effective policies of economic stabilization at the national level—in other words, the space for monetary and fiscal policies to work at all or to work in complementary directions—is defined by the choice of exchange-rate regime and the degree of openness of capital markets.

The conditions of the model at the extreme, conditions such as perfect capital mobility and freely floating exchange rates, have never been met in the real world. But they have sometimes been approached. As circumstances changed in the period following World War II, in fact, different states made different policy choices that are explicable in terms of the Mundell-Fleming model. Monetary autonomy has usually been highly prized, but some states deliberately, albeit not irrevocably, gave it up in order to maintain exchange-rate stability. Austria, for example, tied its monetary policy to its most important trading partner when it anchored the value of the schilling to the German mark and abandoned capital controls. Canada, on the other hand, preferred a flexible exchange rate in order to maintain a degree of monetary policy separation from the United States in an environment of high capital mobility. During the most expansive phase of its postwar boom, Japan adopted a policy line that included a fixed exchange rate, independently managed internal interest rates, and effective capital controls. In the best-known switch in policy priorities, the United States preferred exchange-rate stability and monetary autonomy during the heyday of the Bretton Woods system but abandoned its exchange-rate commitment in the face of capital market pressures in the early 1970s.

Since the early 1970s, the historical record shows that the world's leading industrial states have usually been willing to sacrifice exchange-rate stability when their monetary independence has been threatened by inward or outward capital movements. Their external policies have often been in conflict, but episodes of complete indifference to their exchange rates have been fleeting and ambiguous.[11] The reasons are not hard to locate, and they shed a great deal of light on the noneconomic problem of political legitimacy.

Industrial sectors engaged in trade and international investment account for significant economic growth. The impulse to stabilize exchange rates often arises out of the challenge of maintaining domestic and international political coalitions of sufficient strength to keep national markets open.[12] Although short-term fluctuations in exchange rates do not necessarily compromise the maintenance of such coalitions, longer-term misalignments between major currencies—differences between where real exchange rates actually are and where they should be to promote payments equilibria—threaten to do exactly that.

The historical evidence presented in the next two chapters demonstrates that such a conclusion has long been central to the practice of international monetary diplomacy. Again, the economic theory is straightforward. When trade is free and markets are unhindered, exchange rates should track underlying changes in the purchasing power of national currencies. Nominal exchange rates might fluctuate, but real (price-level-adjusted) exchange rates should be stable. In fact, that stability is often elusive. A high degree of international capital mobility may be one reason. When high mobility exists, changes in exchange rates tend to reflect events and expectations in stock, bond, and other asset markets. Volumes of economic research focus on this issue, but the observation that such markets can and do sometimes move wildly, even irrationally, has never been convincingly dismissed. As domestic prices of goods and services can be sticky, it follows that unpredictable and unstable exchange rates can in principle hurt the real economy by encouraging a misallocation of resources.[13]

Although such a view is commonplace, empirical support is not conclusive. In any event, economists have not been able to find evidence that the most easily measurable costs of exchange-rate instability are high. They have rightly noted, however, a connection between the enduring interest of governments in exchange-rate stability and the challenge governments face in keeping intact the domestic coalitions necessary to support economic openness.[14] When exchange rates are highly unstable, protectionist pressures appear to rise.

In the 1950s and 1960s, leading governments sought to combine the advantages of fixed exchange rates with the capacity to adjust them whenever underlying conditions in national economies warranted such intervention. In theory, the "pegged" exchange rates of the Bretton Woods system depended on a rule-based form of international cooperation, specifically on an interstate legal agreement to collaborate through a multilateral organization—the International Monetary Fund.

The IMF agreement, as we shall see, specified certain rules to guide the exchange-rate policies of its members and gave the organization the power both to sanction changes in exchange rates when required by economic fundamentals and to provide temporary financing in cases where such changes were not required. Governments did not formally have to coordinate their internal monetary and fiscal policies in order to keep their exchange rates stable. In theory, the discipline of exchange-rate rules would automatically promote necessary adjustments in internal policies. In practice, the rules of the game were often honored in the breach, and the IMF was at times ignored. When the system worked, it depended mainly on a low degree of international capital mobility and on the willingness of the United States to keep its import markets open and its domestic price level stable, thereby providing its trading partners with an adequate supply of reserves at reliable value.

The Bretton Woods arrangements collapsed in the early 1970s. Since then, efforts to stabilize exchange rates have taken more limited and sometimes more demanding forms. The gestation of the European Monetary System and the plan for Economic and Monetary Union may be understood in this light. In Mundell-Fleming terms, a successful monetary union depends inevitably upon a willingness by member governments to subordinate the independence of their monetary policies to the common goal of stability in prices and real exchange rates. European monetary union, in particular, amounts to formalizing a type of international cooperation much more rigorous than any contemplated in the Bretton Woods era. National monetary policies will have to be fully coordinated. To ensure that the fundamental goal of those policies is not subverted by divergent fiscal policies, moreover, the actual scope of coordination will have to widen over time.

The same basic impulse, though in a much less demanding form, helps explain occasional efforts during the past two decades to stabilize exchange rates across the world's leading currencies, especially the U.S. dollar, the Japanese yen, and the German mark. The Bonn summit agreement of 1978, the Plaza Agreement of 1985, and the Louvre Accord of 1987, for example, were all attempts to realign exchange rates across the three leading economies by coordinating adjustments in national monetary and fiscal policies. In principle, policy autonomy was sacrificed to the goal of exchange-rate stabilization under conditions of high capital mobility. Such choices, however, rarely lasted very long and almost always proved difficult to implement.

The difficulties either of sustaining multilateral, rule-based collaboration on exchange-rate policies or of designing and carrying through "ad hoc" commitments to coordinate macroeconomic policies convince many economists that governments are unable to pursue optimal strategies, strategies that promise to make everyone better off on the basis of reciprocal adjustments. Some believe that, in aggregate and absolute terms, all would indeed be better off if governments would reliably collaborate on the rules or deliberately coordinate their macroeconomic policies. They also believe, however, that the gains from cheating or from failing to follow through on policy commitments usually overwhelm the incentives to cooperate. In addition, as other economists point out, optimizing strategies tend to be undercut by the fact that an equilibrium exchange rate—the rate at which what a country spends and invests overseas balances what it takes in—is still impossible to estimate with any confidence. In this regard, the IMF itself often and accurately calls attention to "wrong" exchange rates—but has never been able reliably to predict the right one.[15] Similarly, many economists are skeptical of the ability of government officials actually to negotiate paths to optimal national economic performance through coordinated macroeconomic policies. The uncertainties arising from the absence of an agreed model of how real economies adjust to openness, some contend, are still too significant.[16]

Nevertheless, leading states have not shown themselves willing entirely to abandon the goal of exchange-rate stability. The prominent economist Peter Kenen succinctly summarizes the most plausible reason for the occasional episodes of macroeconomic policy coordination witnessed in the years since the Bretton Woods system collapsed:

> Coordination is most likely to occur when governments face a clear and serious threat to the international economic system—an increase in the price of oil like that of the early 1970s, which led to the policy bargain at the 1978 Bonn summit, or

a large exchange rate misalignment like that of the early 1980s, which led to the 1985 Plaza Agreement. When the threat is less obvious or serious, the costs of coordination seem too high, and governments place their national objectives ahead of their global objectives.[17]

In the terms used in Chapter 1, it is easier for governments to combat common evils than to achieve common goods.

Scholars of international relations have devoted considerable attention to the basic theoretical issue here. Their work has shown that strategies of collaboration or coordination among independent states are more likely to develop when those states face dilemmas of common aversions, that is, when they face a common prospect of loss. Dilemmas of common interests might at first seem easier to resolve, but in fact the collaborative behavior required to achieve mutual gains can easily be overwhelmed by desires to avoid relative losses.[18] Simply put, crisis may not be absolutely necessary for international collaboration and coordination, but it does sometimes facilitate them. The irony is that profound crisis can easily have the opposite effect.[19]

A focus on public goods, in contrast to the policy optimization approach, makes it easier to understand the basic Mundell-Fleming trade-off that leading governments have made since the 1970s in their monetary and financial relations with one another. Except for periodic episodes of crisis management, they appear always to have subordinated exchange-rate stability to monetary autonomy and capital mobility. Nevertheless, a modicum of exchange-rate stability remains a shared public good, at least for purposes of grounding liberal trade policies, and so those governments have always been loath to admit their apparent preference.

The Complications of Capital Mobility

In the real world, is it reasonable to assert that the Mundell-Fleming trade-off reflects an *intentional* choice? Do governments actually have the freedom to choose between capital mobility, exchange-rate stability, and monetary autonomy? Or are their choices constrained in very practical ways?

Today, a widespread sense exists that one of those policy options, capital mobility, is no longer subject to choice. At the very least, there is broad acknowledgment of the increasing openness of financial channels across advanced industrial countries and recently across much of the emerging industrial world. National markets in foreign exchange, money market instruments, bank claims, bonds, and stocks are much more open now than they were even a decade ago. The actual magnitude of capital flows through those channels is, nevertheless, still the subject of much empirical analysis and debate, and perfect capital mobility of the kind assumed in the simplest version of the Mundell-Fleming model has never existed.[20]

By the 1990s, however, the perception that capital is much more mobile than it has ever been was firmly embedded in domestic politics across a widening range of countries. In historical terms, as the next chapter demonstrates, this may have been an exaggeration, but there was no denying the political impact of capital market integration in the years following the breakdown of the Bretton Woods exchange-rate system. In fact, the extent of that integration left a growing group of governments with an ever starker choice between exchange-rate stability and national monetary autonomy, a choice that brought to the fore basic concerns about political legitimacy.[21]

"The globalization of finance," a phrase now commonly heard, connotes a number of changes in the world's leading and emerging capital markets. Among the more important are the reduction of direct controls and taxes on financial transactions, the liberalization of long-standing regulatory restrictions on financial intermediaries, the expansion of lightly regulated "offshore" financial markets, and the introduction of new technologies that speed up capital flows and stimulate the development of innovative financial products. All of these developments render capital potentially more mobile, both within and across national frontiers.

Debate on the fundamental political causes of intensifying financial interdependence was in full flower in the early to mid-1990s, both inside and outside the academy.[22] Scholarly research fleshed out explanations at various levels of analysis. Some studies emphasized a competitive, system-level dynamic as states are drawn to the economic stimulus, the jobs, and the raw power promised by expanding national capital markets.[23] Others stressed the conjoined role of liberal ideology and the overwhelming influence of dominant class interests.[24] In a complementary fashion, economic analyses tended to stress the pressures toward openness that arise from technological change and financial innovation.[25] More disaggregated studies depicted expanded financial openness as rooted in unique patterns of domestic politics and in the often unintended consequences of earlier policy decisions.[26]

Simultaneously, researchers probed the consequences of increased financial openness. Some saw it enhancing the risk of global financial crisis and traced the efforts of governments and central banks to contain that risk.[27] Others generally supported the view that the scale and durability of international capital movements are now constitutive of a new regime in world politics, a constraining structure or normative framework increasingly evident in relations among advanced industrial countries and spreading rapidly beyond them.[28] On this view, such a regime lay behind the erosion of extensive welfare programs in the advanced industrial world.[29] It also lay behind the sometimes desperate economic opening of many developing countries.[30] Its underlying norms were widely taken to include currency convertibility, liberal standards of market openness (rights of establishment for foreign institutions and national treatment in regulation after entry), and regulatory transparency.

Relatively open financial markets are not, in fact, new in world politics. Conditions approximating today's "global finance" existed before 1914 among the most advanced economies and their dependencies. The extremities of war and economic depression succeeded in disrupting a system of economic adjustment that accommodated, even necessitated, international capital flows. The system, which dated back to the 1870s, rested on a rough consensus among the principal trading nations. At the center of that consensus lay a version of the gold standard, backed by the wealth and power of Great Britain. In theory, the behavioral norms embedded in the system prescribed relatively passive domestic policy responses to external economic changes. The structure of British financial markets usually provided the key to actual practice. The situation changed completely in 1914.

The tumultuous era that began with World War I witnessed the rise of the modern democratic nation-state, whose citizens expected it to ensure their military security and, increasingly, their economic security.[31] Following the catastrophe of the Great Depression, those national expectations staked out the terrain on which a new intergovernmental consensus on monetary issues was built at Bretton Woods in 1944 and, more fundamentally, on which that consensus evolved in subsequent years. For leading states, as I have already noted, the initial policy mix expressing that consensus privileged exchange-rate stability and limited capital mobility, thereby suppressing any challenge that conditions of interdependence might pose to the autonomy, and ultimately to the legitimacy, of the state itself.

The contemporary reconstruction of global capital markets, or more precisely the dramatic expansion in the capacity of capital to move rapidly across national and regional markets, is intimately linked to the disruption of the Bretton Woods consensus in the 1970s and the dawn of a new era of flexible exchange rates. The expectations of citizens concerning the responsibilities of democratic nation-states appear, however, to have changed substantively. Witness, in this regard, resistance across the advanced industrial world when, during the 1990s, many governments tried to make decisive adjustments in social safety nets. Driven by mounting national debts and deficits, as well as a return to the orthodoxy of the early twentieth century regarding their consequences, a broad attempt was made to trim the sails of the welfare state, if not to cut down the masts altogether. The next chapter discusses the earlier manifestation of that orthodoxy in more detail. It is sufficient here to note what it meant for an increasing number of governments as the 1990s progressed.

Though it was not yet perfected by the early 1990s, the tendency toward a new Mundell-Fleming trade-off was quite widely observable. Across the leading countries—the United States, Germany, and Japan—international capital mobility and national monetary autonomy were accorded priority. The necessary consequence was acceptance of flexible exchange rates. Only inside Europe was another set of priorities explicitly debated, if not yet fully enshrined in practice. As members of the European Monetary System attempted to move toward full monetary union, they evidently began to consider monetary autonomy secondary to open capital markets and stable exchange rates.

Across Europe, North America, and much of East Asia, nonetheless, the priority now assigned to capital mobility was striking. Although, again, this was not unprecedented in modern history, it *was* unprecedented to combine such a priority with states' acceptance of political responsibility for the broadly defined security of their citizens. Never before had the Mundell-Fleming preference for international capital mobility, national or regional monetary autonomy, and flexible exchange rates had to confront the exigencies of what many were now calling the entitlement state.

As the twentieth century came to a close, economic commentators, prominent bankers, and conservative politicians, often abstracting from the fact that governments can let their exchange rates float, underscored the "discipline" on autonomous state action implied by international capital mobility. If that discipline entailed cutting back on the welfare supports and entitlements of the era since 1945, they asserted, then so be it. Many of their opponents on the left may have rejected the conclusion, but they intuitively understood its logic. Indeed, a mounting body of popular literature written by both conservatives and radicals in the 1990s envisaged the consolidation of a new global order, the borderless order of advanced capitalism.[32]

Whether observers embraced it or loathed it, such a vision was informed by a materialist worldview, and the language that invoked it was the language of inevitability. Costs and benefits were measurable, and the costs of closure outweighed any benefits imaginable. Enjoining governments to yield to signals from the "global market," the language of capital mobility implied that a profound shift in policymaking authority was necessarily taking place, a shift away from the national level. Proponents typically extolled the surrender of the retrograde idea of "sovereignty" to the rational economic logic of markets beyond national control. Opponents may not have liked such a conclusion, but their own research bolstered the notion that transnational coalitions beyond the state now exercised determinative influence over a widening range of economic policies.

If sovereignty is defined as policy autonomy, and it is common to do so, then international capital mobility seems necessarily to imply a loss of sovereignty. Unfortunately, such a narrow definition ignores both an extensive literature on the legal concept of sovereignty and a generation of research on the political trade-offs implied by international economic interdependence.[33] Conflating policy autonomy and sovereignty also downplays the stark historical lesson of 1914 and 1939: conditions of crisis, especially catastrophic crisis, reveal the locus of ultimate political authority in the modern age— the state. To put the matter bluntly, if states are willing to bear the costs, they can still opt out of the emergent regime of capital mobility. Abrogation of that regime itself by the collectivity of states may not be desirable, but it is certainly not inconceivable. As long as that remains the case, states retain their sovereignty.

In practical terms, nevertheless, many states today do confront tighter constraints on economic policy as a consequence of freer flows of capital across their borders. Again, the phenomenon itself is not new. What is new is the widespread perception that all states, all societies, all social groups are now affected. In light of the historical record, such a perception is wrong. Most important, it blurs critical distinctions between and within states. Underneath the overt discourse on "sovereignty" and capital mobility lies a covert discourse on power, legitimacy, and hierarchy.

If effective governing authority has been usurped by global capital markets, or if such authority has surreptitiously been devolved to those markets by governments themselves, then surely questions are raised about how such a shift has taken place and about the obligation of citizens to comply. Today there is only one place where such questions can be directed and satisfactorily addressed. And whether we conceive of it as an arena, a structure, or a set of institutions, that place is called the state.

The Mundell-Fleming trade-off tells us a great deal about the internal choices states make when they seek to harness the benefits of economic openness without incurring unacceptable costs. The sum of those choices over the past two decades is behind the international capital markets of today. But those markets were not built by economic happenstance. They reflect a political project that was shaped by the domestic priorities and external strategies of leading states. International economic institutions are an important part of that project. In order to come to grips with the most fundamental role of the institution at the center of this book, we need first to see today's capital markets in their historical context.

International Institutions and the Capital Markets

Early in the period between the two great wars of the twentieth century, leading states tried with an increasing sense of urgency to craft a global economy. During the 1920s, as we shall see in the next chapter, general consensus was achieved at the level of principle. A bulwark of peace lay within reach if that consensus, which today we would label classically liberal and which hinged on a workable gold standard and more open capital markets, could be put into practice. The effort failed, and it failed catastrophically.

After World War II, leading states again attempted to restore economic openness, but this time on a foundation of preponderant American military power and the modified economic principles noted in Chapter 1. On that basis, deepening international economic integration was intimately linked with the domestic politics of the welfare state. After the Cold War began, the military calculation became more complex, but economic *and* financial openness moved to the center of the foreign policies of advanced industrial states. Outside the Communist bloc, the principle attracted a growing international constituency. Adherents never made stark and irrevocable decisions to favor financial openness above all other economic objectives, but they did adjust a widening range of internal policies to promote and accommodate potentially more extensive flows of capital across national borders. They also reshaped the mandates of international institutions in this light.

From the late 1940s to the early 1970s leading states, once again in Mundell-Fleming terms, moved away from one set of policy trade-offs and toward another. After World War II, they sought both exchange-rate stability and monetary autonomy, and they were willing to tolerate limits on capital mobility in order to achieve those objectives. As that system was breaking down, they gave priority to capital mobility and monetary autonomy and were willing to abandon exchange-rate stability. Note that only one priority remained constant. Still held responsible for national security, broadly defined—and in practice defined by interest-group politics in combination with general electoral demands for satisfactory macroeconomic performance—states retained the right to craft internal monetary policies as they themselves saw fit. In short, the abandonment of exchange-rate stability and the privileging of international capital mobility were ways of exporting some of the effects of uncoordinated national policies.

After the breakdown of the exchange-rate mechanism of the Bretton Woods system, which we shall explore later, states collectively encouraged the further expansion of international capital movements. They did so even as some of them, mainly in Europe, sought to restore a degree of exchange-rate stability for themselves by limiting their own monetary autonomy within regional or bilateral arrangements. Sometimes they encouraged capital flows through direct policy actions designed to liberate market forces, finance budget and trade deficits, or respond to competitive threats from other states. At other times, they did so by *not* taking decisions, such as decisions to subject financial transactions between banks and their foreign customers to the same sorts of reserve requirements and taxes routinely imposed on purely domestic transactions.

Having set in motion a system that lacked a reliable mechanism for pegging currency values, leading states subsequently found that further capital liberalization, combined with enhanced market supervision, was in political terms less costly than an attempt to resurrect the Bretton Woods system. To be sure, many other states continued to rely on capital controls to buffer their national economies. In the wake of disruptive bouts of capital flight in various industrializing countries, for example, such controls sometimes were acquiesced in by other states and by the IMF. But approval, whether formal or tacit, was almost always conditional on an understanding that controls would be temporary. From the late 1970s through the mid-1990s, capital decontrol came ever more clearly to define a basic norm of the international economy.

Let us be clear on this crucial point. Even in the 1990s, capital flows continued to encounter "frictions" at national borders. That is, there has yet to arise a truly global financial market characterized by perfect capital mobility and structural homogeneity.[34] Nevertheless, governmental policies formerly accommodated the possibility, even at times the necessity, of controls on short-term capital movements; during the past two decades they have converged in the direction of liberalization. Such convergent policies, and a consequent reorientation of the expectations of state and market actors, suggest a fundamental break with the original Bretton Woods consensus. In 1989 that convergence was recognized by member countries of the OECD, when they widened the scope of the Capital Movements Code. Although escape clauses were retained, the subsequent activism of the OECD in working to minimize the reservations of member-states suggests an attempt by leading members to replace the formal legal right to control capital movements with a new right.

The effort to codify the norm of capital mobility continues. The reluctance of states unambiguously to embrace it, even as their own policies advance its cause, suggests a deeper concern. The legal issue masks an issue of power and authority. The legitimacy of the new order remains in question. More fundamentally, the struggle suggests that the architects of that order cannot easily calibrate emergent market facts with political realities. They cannot lodge ultimate political authority over international capital markets at the level where it logically belongs. Nation-states are now like subnational governments in a confederation ostensibly trying to establish a fully integrated national market while retaining all substantive economic powers themselves. They have a problem. The legitimation of truly global capital markets appears to entail the delegitimation of their own authority.

International Oversight and Integrating Markets

The states that took the first steps in structuring the postwar monetary and financial system did make one novel commitment. That political commitment deepened policy linkages among them far beyond those that characterized, for example, the trading partnership between Germany and Great Britain before the great wars of the twentieth century. It signaled a significant and basic normative change. The custom and practice of international economic diplomacy had not typically attempted to confront the internal policy choices made by states, particularly leading states. The notion of international legal obligation was generally restricted to relations beyond the domestic. World War II, however, prompted a sea change. As the distinguished scholar Robert Cox put it, that notion moved "to a general recognition that measures of national economic policy affect other countries and that such consequences should be taken into account before national policies are adopted."[35] This normative change opened the door to the principle of international oversight.

The most obvious of the policies requiring objective monitoring, and perhaps the easiest to subject to external accountability without engendering immediate and negative domestic political reactions, involved the exchange rate. In this obscure domain of aloof finance ministers and central bankers, what would eventually develop into the institutionally most robust version of international oversight was initiated.

As later chapters explain, states formalized their commitment to the principle of multilateral oversight when they re-constituted the IMF in the 1970s.[36] Unwilling to accept the domestic strictures of a fixed exchange-rate system, and willing to risk a high degree of exchange-rate instability, they nevertheless endeavored to enhance the openness in national payment systems deemed essential to the expansion of international trade and investment. Over time, developments in financial markets accelerated policy adjustments. But those markets themselves did not come out of nowhere. They were collective political creations.

Exchange-rate policies are inherently difficult to separate from monetary policies more generally. To recapitulate, interest rates, inflation rates, and exchange rates are in practice intimately related. Moreover, a range of other policies—from basic fiscal policies to various structural and regulatory policies—have an impact on all of these variables. And that impact cannot easily be contained when currencies are readily convertible and payment systems are open. In short, an exchange rate encapsulates a large number of choices made about national economic policy. Policy boundaries around the IMF would therefore necessarily blur and expand as the Fund evolved. Although an array of institutional competitors would also develop, one mandate provided the essential rationale for the expansion over time of the Fund's operations.

The Fund continues to rest on the principle that member-states are accountable to one another for the external effects of their domestic economic policies. The fact that these effects are now being transmitted more rapidly through deepening international financial markets explains the gradual extension of the Fund's mandate beyond exchange rate policies narrowly conceived. Conversely, the limits on that role, both legal and customary, signal the essential imperfection of those markets.

The legal obligation entailed in the Fund's central mandate nevertheless established from its inception a normative presumption of intensive international collaboration, which in turn conferred meaning on formerly unencumbered acts. Nothing, however, precluded breaches. If acceptance of an obligation is serious, breaches call forth rationalization and explanation. Significant and continual breaches without acceptable explanation destroy the underlying norm. Despite the vast changes represented by the reprioritization of the goals of exchange-rate stability and international capital mobility recounted above, this is precisely what did *not* happen to the fundamental presumption of collaborative behavior ever since World War II.

Exchange rates, the variables most immediately reflective of economic interdependence, provided the initial focus of underlying obligation, and the central institutional mechanism for overseeing compliance was embodied in the IMF. In the pegged exchange-rate system designed at Bretton Woods in 1944, the oversight role of the Fund was in principle critical. As we shall see, however, in practice the Fund's real responsibilities were limited, and significant room remained for autonomous national policymaking. At any particular point in time exchange rates were to be fixed, but over time they were also to be adjustable in the face of "fundamental" disequilibria in payments balances. In theory, Fund approval was required for changes in exchange-rate parities. The Fund also had a role to play in encouraging member-states that maintained exchange restrictions on their current accounts to move toward liberalization. Currency convertibility and open national payment systems were to be the handmaidens of expanding world trade, and Fund oversight was to encourage attendant adjustments in national policies. The Fund, in short, was to be a source of policy "discipline."

It turned out that private markets, especially private capital markets, would play this role more effectively, at least for some countries. Partly for this reason, one needs to delve only briefly into the literature to discern a widespread skepticism, especially with respect to the policies of leading states, concerning what came to be called Fund surveillance. As many scholarly and popular commentators have noted, the advice resulting from surveillance activities can be controversial and is frequently ignored, not only by great powers but by smaller states as well.[37] For the former group, IMF surveillance and its analogs in the OECD and elsewhere rest on no practical power to impose sanctions. For the latter, enforcement is sometimes but not always enhanced if a state is in desperate financial straits and policy advice flowing out of surveillance procedures can be transformed into "conditions" attached to loans.

In truth, dissatisfaction with the practice of multilateral surveillance has deepened since Susan Strange labeled the Fund's version a "pantomime" in the early 1970s.[38] Although supporters persist in depicting it as a harbinger of future collective governance for an integrated global economy, they bemoan its limitations. Critics on both the right and the left, conversely, depict it as a cover for the exercise of arbitrary power by leading states, or as a more insidious threat to responsible democratic government.[39] Some of its right-wing opponents would like to see it replaced by a less politicized mechanism for subjecting national economic policies to the pressures of interdependence, as might be imagined in a functioning gold- or commodity-based monetary system.[40] Others wistfully recall an era when national economies could contemplate a higher degree of policy autonomy. A more common criticism of multilateral economic surveillance in practice is built into the worldviews of enthusiastic supporters of expanding global capital markets. Those markets, we now commonly hear, force national policy adjustments in a way that the surveillance of intergovernmental institutions can never match.[41]

Despite such criticism and dissatisfaction, substantial financial, intellectual, and political resources are devoted to multilateral economic surveillance in general and to the surveillance function of the IMF in particular. The Fund's surveillance mandate, indeed, is today at the very core of the institution.[42] All Fund members now participate in regular, obligatory consultations with the staff. Staff reports, in turn, form the basis for formal "decisions" of the Fund's board on the appropriateness of national economic policies or the advisability of certain changes. More generally, analytical staff of the Fund, the managing director, and the Executive Board provide overall systemic surveillance. The most visible manifestation of that work is regularly published studies meant to help shape the development of relevant national policies. Directly or indirectly, all Fund policies relate back to its surveillance function. Most of the time of most Fund staff members is devoted to the process, whether or not Fund loans are involved. Similarly in the Group of Seven, the OECD, the Bank for International Settlements, and the European Union, member-states regularly subject their policies to the scrutiny of their partners.

If the surveillance exercises of the Fund and its analogs are a waste of time and energy, then senior policymakers owe a substantial explanation to their constituents. If surveillance really is useful for its ostensible purposes, those same constituents should have witnessed in recent decades less exchange-rate misalignment across major currencies, and in general more consistent macroeconomic policies.

At various times as governments have discussed international monetary reform since the 1970s, multilateral surveillance could have been given more substance. It could also have been abandoned. As we shall see, however, at moments of decision policymakers in the leading states have continually reaffirmed the kind of commitment originally made at Bretton Woods and sharpened in 1975 through the Fund's amended Articles of Agreement. They have yet to abrogate the principle that they are accountable to other states for their internal economic choices. Indeed, over time they have allowed the actual practice of surveillance by the Fund to become more intrusive. Still focused mainly on macroeconomic policies, multilateral surveillance in practice increasingly encompasses structural and microeconomic policies, including the regulation of capital movements. Among the states of the European Union, the significant strengthening of its regional analog, a binding macroeconomic surveillance mechanism, is at the forefront of an ambitious agenda whose ultimate aim is the construction of a single market with a common currency.[43]

If the principle behind multilateral economic surveillance is meaningful, why have states not transferred substantive authority to strong international organizations? If, on the other hand, the principle is vapid, why have they not simply abandoned it?

Recall the spectrums of theoretical possibilities introduced in Chapter 1 for addressing the fundamental tension between the conflicting logics of markets and politics. The following chapters trace a vital aspect of the long, twentieth-century struggle to avoid the two ends of the economic spectrum. Intentionally dis-integrated national financial markets on the one side; on the other, stable global markets resting on adequate instruments of global governance, were, and remain, anathema. States, especially leading states, have demonstrated clear interests in capturing the benefits of deepening financial market integration *without* fundamentally compromising their ultimate political authority over that process.

After World War II, and in marked contrast to the interwar experience, the United States and its principal allies came to see international organizations as important instruments for managing the tension between integrating markets and decentralized governance. The path along which the IMF and its analogs have developed since then has not been straight and narrow. Politics, choice, and the ever-present threat of financial crisis have charted its course.

The Fund is emblematic of the loose political regime thereby constituted. Its endurance and the rearticulation of its principal mandate over time are best understood against the backdrop of the legitimacy problem posed for states by their broader collective choice to advance the cause of international financial integration. At a minimum, that choice enhanced the possibility that financial crises would spill over national borders. At a maximum, it promised accelerated economic growth. For smaller states seeking such growth, it also appeared to render it increasingly difficult to diverge from economic standards set within the economies of leading states.

The trade-offs for economic policy implied in the assignment of priority to international capital mobility were recognized in 1944. Even clearer to the architects of the Bretton Woods system was the associated political conundrum. Capital mobility combined with stable exchange rates could undermine the authority of the state itself by compromising its ability to train its most powerful economic instruments on domestic priorities. Moreover, no other political agency capable of legitimately wielding that authority existed. Before we explore how contemporary states are attempting to deal with the same fundamental political dilemma, we need to go back to a time much earlier in the twentieth century, when the architects of international economic and financial integration thought they had the answer. In many ways, their attempt to build a solid political and institutional base for the restoration of global finance foreshadowed our own. The next two chapters explore the long-forgotten experiment to create a legitimate, effective instrument for global economic oversight in the League of Nations. That experiment failed in its own time, but it casts new light on ours.

CHAPTER 3

The League of Nations and the Roots of Multilateral Oversight

*T*HE VERY NAME "LEAGUE OF NATIONS" HAS BECOME A METAPHOR for failure. In the wake of the war it was originally designed to prevent, the League became the example that the architects of new multilateral institutions tried to avoid. Perhaps it is not surprising, then, that our textbooks in international relations and international economics commonly leave the impression that the international organizations established after World War II were entirely new departures in history.

Despite the well-documented contribution of the British delegation at the 1944 Bretton Woods conference, and the less well-known input of the Canadians, the now conventional view is that the IMF and its sister organizations, including the World Bank and the antecedent to the World Trade Organization (WTO), reflected a fresh, novel American vision for international economic relations. In this and other policy areas, the title of Secretary of State Dean Acheson's memoirs, *Present at the Creation,* summed up the worldview of a generation of American policymakers and scholars. The global conflagration that began in the 1930s erased what had gone before. The Americans, with a little help from their friends, were painting on a blank canvas.[1]

The United States was indeed more than the first among equals after the war, but the postwar experiment in building international economic institutions was not entirely novel. Largely forgotten in the conventional view is the economic work of the League of Nations. This chapter traces the development of key aspects of that work during the 1920s, and the next carries the story through to 1945, when the League ceased to exist. As we shall see, World War II was not the watershed that many now take it to be. The League was deeply implicated in the first attempt in the twentieth century to restore global finance, and in this regard its monetary and financial activities foreshadowed the core mandate of the International Monetary Fund. The League eventually proved an ill-suited vehicle for managing the legitimacy problem posed by a widening disjunction between national politics and international economics in the interwar period. Nonetheless, its activities and its ultimate failure influenced the Fund's mandate in some surprisingly direct ways.

The Economic and Financial Organization of the League

The standard history of the League of Nations barely mentions its economic activities.[2] This lacuna may partly be explained by the fact that the original architects of the League never explicitly intended the organization to develop as an economic actor.[3] Only Articles 22 and 23 of the League's Covenant actually mention economic matters, and there only in very specific contexts.[4] That formal committees, special councils, and a secretariat began to develop on this basis testifies less to their legal foundation than to the nature of the problems encountered by member-states in the years after the Armistice. Functions developed from practice as leading members assigned specific tasks to the League.

Part of the League's secretariat evolved into the Economic, Financial, and Transit Department (Section). Walter Layton and then Frank

Nixon were the first directors, soon to be followed by Arthur Salter, who served as permanent director from 1922 until 1931. Like the League's secretary general, Eric Drummond, all were British nationals. Members of the department in the early years included Jean Monnet from France, Per Jacobsson from Sweden, and Alexander Loveday from Britain, who headed the self-contained Economic Intelligence Service.[5] The department was split in 1931 into its various components, with Loveday taking over the financial and economic intelligence work and Pietro Stoppani of Italy heading the economic section. In 1938, all of the sections were merged again, under Loveday.

The staff worked under the broad guidance of the League's Assembly, which included a few ministers of commerce and finance, and the more specific direction of standing committees of the Council, which was mainly comprised of foreign ministers. Economic, Financial, Fiscal, and Statistical committees were established, and all later operated separately or jointly. As a result, the work of the staff was not always clearly bounded. As we shall see, some worked mainly on what we would today call macroeconomic issues, but many moved fluidly across policy terrain that is now split among such organizations as the IMF, the World Bank, and the World Trade Organization. In addition, and often quite extensively, outside experts and special-purpose committees complemented the work of the staff. Before World War II broke out, sixty-five League staffers worked exclusively on economic and financial matters, and their operations became known as the Economic and Financial Organization (EFO) of the League.[6] Almost all worked in Geneva until the summer of 1940, when forty took up residence at the Institute for Advanced Study in Princeton, New Jersey.

Much like their descendants in the IMF today, spokesmen for the EFO always portrayed themselves as "technicians" involved in "technical" problems. Again like the IMF, however, the actual mandate of the Organization turned out to be expansive and profoundly political. Perhaps for this reason, the work was perceived by many to be simultaneously exhilarating and frustrating. As its first director remarked to his successor in 1922, "the chances of its being able to do any really useful work [were] so poor that it should be reduced to the smallest dimensions and put into cold storage for an indefinite time."[7] Many years later, Louis Rasminsky, who joined the EFO in 1930 and played a significant role in establishing the IMF during the next decade, put the matter more prosaically: "At the League, we were expected to catch fish, but we had no bait."[8] Between those years, however, there were times of hope, even optimism.

Liberal Dreams: The Brussels Conference and the Inception of Multilateral Oversight

The seeds of multilateral economic oversight, the incipient mandate of what would become the EFO and the harbinger of what we now call economic surveillance, were sown in Brussels during the International Financial Conference of 1920. The economies of Europe were then in extreme distress. Industrial and agricultural production had been devastated by the war and its chaotic aftermath, trade was being throttled as bankrupt governments desperately tried to raise revenues and protect domestic producers through increasing tariffs, banking systems were in disarray, foreign credit was inadequate to jump-start the process of reconstruction, and ruinous inflationary spirals had been unleashed. In such circumstances, thirty-nine countries responded to a call from the League for a conference to consider the impasse and suggest ways out. Nominated by their governments, delegates were to attend in their private capacities.[9] This arrangement testified to the immensity of the task, from which governments desired some distance, but the maneuver also allowed non-members of the League, including the United States, to attend.[10]

In retrospect, it is easy to downplay the results of the Brussels Conference. Lacking substantive authority, the declarations of its expert groups were obviously hortatory. Nonetheless, the delegates reached a remarkably broad consensus on the principles appropriate to guide national policies. With regard to internal policy goals, the delegates appealed to governments to return to those of the prewar era. Governments should balance their budgets and restore credibility to their currencies by disinflating. "The country which accepts the policy of budget deficits," the delegates collectively intoned in words that reverberate today, "is treading the slippery slope to general ruin; to escape from that path, no sacrifice is too great."[11] Not so often heard today, however, was the corollary:

> To enable governments to give effect to the principle of sound finance, all classes of the community must contribute their share. All classes of the population and particularly the wealthy must be prepared willingly to accept the charges necessary to remedy the present situation. . . . Fresh taxation must be imposed to meet the deficit.[12]

With regard to exchange rates, most histories of the conference have reported an appeal for a return to the gold standard. It is true that delegates cited the stability associated with a viable gold standard as an ideal to be achieved. They stated, however, that a return to the gold standard should not be attempted before countries were ready. Internal financial stability was required before the gold standard could be restored.[13] The delegates made other recommendations, including one calling for the abolition of "artificial" restraints on trade. Finally, they requested the Secretariat of the League to report on the actual responses of governments to all of their recommendations.

That report was released in 1922.[14] Drafted on the basis of a coherent set of principles, it set down an important marker. No great leap of the imagination is required to see in it the precursor of the world economic surveys that the IMF and its sister agencies now regularly compile and publish in fulfillment of their own systemic oversight roles. In light of what was to happen in the 1930s it is easy, of course, to be cynical about the utility of the 1922 report and the process that initiated it. But how did it look to contemporaries? As one close observer recalled, twenty-five years after the Brussels Conference:

> The recommendations exercised a powerful influence on governments and expert opinion in the ensuing years; they were applied by the League in its various schemes for the financial reconstruction of individual countries; they also provided a standard of financial orthodoxy to which appeal was constantly

made in the course of the subsequent painful and difficult process of restoring budgetary and currency stability and reopening the channels of international trade. This was the real achievement of the Conference.[15]

Of course, what really matters is not what governments said but what they did. In the 1920s, some would at least try to put the principles into practice. In essence, as we shall see, this meant attempting to undergird the legitimacy of states and their economic policies, to give confidence to international markets, and in this way to help restore the world torn asunder in 1914. Though not the instigator, the League became a central instrument in the pursuit of that objective.

Developing Core Principles: The Genoa Conference of 1922

As is the case today with the IMF, the oversight function of the League initiated by the Brussels Conference took two distinct forms. The first was analytical and balanced; symmetry was sought in the rhetorical application of principled guidance to all countries.[16] The second applied those principles more forcefully. It finds its contemporary analog in the conditional financing facilities the Fund makes available to countries in difficult straits. Central European countries received similar assistance from the League during the early 1920s. Before turning to those seminal events, we need to consider the elaboration of the Brussels principles, which took place at the first major postwar economic conference attended by heads of government.

At the Paris Peace Conference in January 1922, the principal Allied powers invited the heads of government of the former Axis powers and the Soviet Union to meet at Genoa the following April to resolve outstanding economic and financial issues left over since the Armistice. Technically, the Genoa Conference was not held under the auspices of the League of Nations, thus permitting the formal participation of the United States and the Soviet Union.[17] And although there were noteworthy developments on the economic side of the conference agenda, all coordinated in fact by the Secretariat of the League, the most important items on the agenda were deeply intertwined with vital questions of military security.[18]

In the end, the Genoa Conference would signify the beginning of the end of the League's experiment in collective security. It nevertheless did manage to adopt three major reports submitted by special commissions of the League. The reports concerned economic, financial, and transportation issues. Very much like analogous studies today published routinely by the IMF and its sister organizations, the three reports were agenda-setting, "big-picture" pieces. Didactic in style and liberal in tone, they contained numerous recommendations for reforms in government policies.[19] For our purposes, the most interesting was the report of the Financial Commission.

In essence, the report elaborated on the principles first articulated two years earlier at Brussels.[20] Instead of concentrating on the internal macroeconomic requirements for financial stabilization, however, it focused on the microeconomic foundations of economic recovery and growth. The Commission was headed by the British chancellor of the exchequer, and its report bore the marks of the main commissioners, all leading British, American, German, Dutch, and Swedish bankers.

The report called for an end to "futile and mischievous" exchange controls. It decried political interference in the business of banking and called for greater autonomy for central banks. Among those banks it recommended cooperation on a full range of issues, the most important of which was the restoration of a functioning gold standard. In this regard, the report proposed a novel plan for doing so without unduly impairing world liquidity; the strongest countries would hold their reserves in gold, whereas others could hold reserves in the form of the convertible currencies of those countries.[21] The report also recommended an in-depth study by the League on the interrelated issues of capital flight, tax evasion, and double taxation. Finally, it opposed intergovernmental loans and write-offs of governmentally sponsored debt in principle and advocated private refinancing of existing governmental debts. Exactly how this might be done, especially given the politically untenable weight of German reparations and outstanding Soviet debt, was left unspecified.[22]

These recommendations did not, of course, stand alone and there were reasons deeper than ideology for their orthodoxy. Conceptually and politically, there was no way the restoration of the freer flow of international commerce could occur in the absence of stable currency markets. Beyond governments standing behind the "sanctity of contracts," no one had any real idea how to ensure stability in the wake of all-too-imaginable defaults by the Soviets, the Germans, and others sure to follow.

It became apparent in the debate at Genoa that without the financial stability that delegates imagined would eventually result from a restored gold or gold-exchange standard and well-functioning private capital markets, there could be no consensus on the central recommendation embodied in the companion Economic Report: namely, that national commercial polices should be reconstituted around the principle of nondiscrimination. Also called the most-favored-nation principle, it required that trade concessions made to one partner be extended to all others. France and Spain, in particular, feared that intentional currency depreciation and capital mobility in combination with nondiscriminatory trade policies would devastate their economies. In the words of one observer, "The pervasive factor of currency instability was mainly responsible for the continued enforcement of import prohibitions and restrictions in many European countries, those with weak currencies seeking thereby to strengthen their balance of payments position, the others anxious to guard against exchange dumping." [23] Export controls to protect agricultural supplies and raw materials had a similar effect. Financial stability must come first, and on that point the conference achieved consensus.

The fundamental problem remained intractable. How could the impulse to adopt protective domestic policies accommodate the desire to recover the international economy of the prewar era? To have retreated from such policies, however, would have called into question the legitimacy of the state itself, an issue that was far from academic at a time when a growing communist movement gave focus to just such dilemma.

With no shared understanding of the principled foundations for compatible commercial policies, politicians could never be confident that financial stabilization—even if it could be engineered through private financial markets—would initiate a virtuous cycle of reconstruction and growth across Europe. Without such a consensus, it would continue to be logical, even necessary, for countries to husband all possible future bargaining chips on trade and to cooperate with one another only on matters for which an unambiguous domestic rationale existed.[24] Financial stabilization in itself had such a rationale, and few politicians saw much reason to disrupt the collective understandings of the bankers. Only if and when the bankers failed would governments have to clarify their priorities. Helping them not to fail was therefore important. The first test would come as various Central European countries approached the financial brink.

Imperfect though they would turn out to be in their broader application, the liberal principles developed in Genoa guided the League as it grappled with various national debt crises during the mid-1920s. Its incipient multilateral oversight role was signified in the background work and final economic reports accepted at Genoa. But little practical effect could be claimed until the chance came to apply those principles directly, in Central Europe.

The Financial Reconstruction of Central Europe

The refinancing of Austria in 1923 is usually recorded as the first debt-workout case involving the League. In fact, it was the second. Historians and memoirists of the League have missed an earlier event. According to a memorandum written by a senior League staffer in August 1922, the League assisted earlier that year with a loan floated on international capital markets for the country then called Czecho-Slovakia. To assure repayment, the lead investment banker, Baring Brothers, had demanded the right directly to control the administration of customs and tariff receipts pledged as security, a condition that earlier had been successfully imposed on Turkey. Czecho-Slovakia refused to accede. A compromise was struck on the basis of a suggestion from the borrower that the League be appointed arbitrator in case of future disputes; in the event of difficulty with the loan's security, the League would be empowered to "take such action as might be necessary to secure the interest of the bond holders." The agreement was subsequently ratified by both the lending syndicate (which included a predecessor to Citibank of the United States) and the Council of the League. As the League staffer involved put it, "Evidently, the reason why this kind of arrangement is acceptable to the [Prague] government is that Czecho-Slovakia is a member of the League and she is not, therefore, sacrificing her independence or diminishing her sovereignty in accepting [League] jurisdiction."[25]

As the first case implies, there were substantial differences in the precise modalities through which funds for economic stabilization could be provided, in the early 1920s as in analogous situations today. Unlike the IMF, the League had no funds of its own, and with intergovernmental lending frowned on in principle, any significant external financing had to come from private capital markets. In later cases in which the League would be much more actively engaged, its main contribution would be to provide the sort of political buffer it supplied in the case of Czecho-Slovakia.

In the Austrian case, the country's marketable assets were already encumbered by foreign liens, and the reparations payments imposed in the aftermath of the Armistice were crushing. Hyperinflation was by now institutionalized. As a senior League official noted during his first visit in 1922, office clerks were using Austrian crown notes as scribbling paper; the cheapest paper they could get, it cost sixty times its face value to print.[26] The broader human consequences are well documented. Famine was abroad in the land, and Austrian society was on the edge of the abyss. In this context, fractious political debate was beginning to center, once again, on the idea that the only road to survival was the one that led to Berlin. The victorious Allies had long ago come to fear just such an outcome. Having vetoed union in 1919, they subsequently used both public and private charitable routes to pump emergency financing into the Austrian economy.

Britain had built up the largest exposure. By 1922, however, neither the British, French, nor American governments were willing to pump in more. The governor of the Bank of England advised the British Cabinet that the effects of total financial collapse in Austria could be contained. The Cabinet agreed "that no useful purpose would be served by advancing further financial assistance to the Austrian Government merely with a view to postponing what appeared to be an inevitable financial catastrophe."[27] An inter-Allied conference was convened in London on August 7 and the decision to stop further loans was taken. One further decision followed. On August 15, the task of dealing with the consequences was handed over to the League.[28] As one historian reflected on that latter decision:

> What the Allied powers seemed to be doing and probably thought they were doing was washing their hands of Austria and leaving the League to take whatever opprobrium was going when the country broke up. Prudent voices advised the Council of the League to have nothing to do with it, because the certain failure of Austria must harm the League. But the Council took it on.[29]

In the event, the Council struck a special "Austria Committee," comprising key foreign ministers and the Austrian chancellor. Under its direction, the Secretariat worked out a plan of action, which elaborated a concrete program for currency reform proposed by British Treasury officials. After much delay, the result was a £26 million loan raised in private markets, guaranteed by eight European governments, and administered directly in Vienna by a commissioner appointed by the League. In practice, the League commissioner, assisted by Arthur Salter and other members of the Secretariat, would personally supervise the flow of customs revenues and other foreign exchange through government coffers for three and a half years.[30] Without that power, lenders could not be confident that their loan would be repaid.

The memory of Commissioner-General Alfred Zimmermann, a Dutch national and former mayor of Rotterdam, remains vivid in Austrian financial circles, not so much for his role in saving the country as for his extraordinary lack of tact. Nevertheless, that role gave him considerable influence over Austrian economic policy. How could the League ensure that such influence would not be perceived as arbitrary? League staff envisaged three methods. Zimmermann's advice would have to be consistent with general principles acknowledged as applicable to all countries. He would have to leave as soon as possible. And he would have to be thoroughly versed in the arts of diplomacy. In the event, the first two proved sufficient to the specific task.

The basic principles of financial stabilization articulated at the Brussels Conference and developed at the Genoa Conference were applied, and the intervention worked despite Dr. Zimmermann's heavy-handedness.[31] He left after forty-two months. The loan was repaid, the currency stabilized, and the national budget balanced. A process of reconstruction had begun. No one could then foresee that it would all collapse in 1931, or that the League itself would be destroyed by the forces then unleashed.

Hailed as the League's first practical achievement, the Austrian loan was followed by another in 1924, to a desperate Hungary. Under the terms of a program modeled on the Austrian experiment, a £10 million (unguaranteed) infusion accomplished the same result. A League-appointed commissioner acted, in effect, as the agent for the note-holders, administered the program directly in Budapest, and left after two years.[32]

Subsequently, League staff offered minor technical assistance based on the Austrian and Hungarian successes to Estonia, the free city of Danzig, and Portugal.[33] But those experiences seemed to involve a stigma that discouraged others from associating with the League. Perhaps more important, political differences among leading states ensured that the League would never extend its principles or its oversight to the most sensitive and significant debtor countries, especially Poland and Germany.[34] As Arthur Salter put it, somewhat too delicately:

By [the late 1920s] the very fame of the League's action entailed disadvantages. It led to the belief that the appropriate clients for the League were countries who were completely down and out and who both needed, and would be required to accept, the same onerous and rather humiliating form of control for a period. Other countries therefore . . . , while profiting from the technical experience gained in the League's experiments, preferred to make direct arrangements with foreign issuing houses and to carry reforms through without any impairment of national responsibility beyond what might be imposed by the lenders.[35]

Substitute "IMF" for "League," and few would be surprised to see Salter's words applied to the contemporary period. Authoritative oversight by a multilateral institution, though preferable to direct intrusion by another state, would never be enthusiastically welcomed by recipients. As we shall see, however, many of those countries came back to the League when they sank into debt crises in the early 1930s. Once again, such developments would bring to light the role of a collaborative political mechanism underneath ostensibly private international markets. It would also underline a basic paradox. The actions of states could easily destabilize such markets; when those markets functioned well, it was states and the agencies they created that provided the confidence without which they could not function at all. In the late 1920s, however, the dream that politics could somehow be removed from markets, that those markets could underpin themselves, lived on.

Liberal Orthodoxy Resurgent: League Oversight at the End of the 1920s

Buoyed by the unexpected successes of the Austrian and Hungarian stabilizations, members of the League's Assembly began talking in 1925 of an international economic conference. Unlike the Genoa Conference, this one would be formally sponsored by the League and would concentrate on economic issues. The aim was to consolidate a consensus on policy settings required for prosperity. "Economic peace will largely contribute to security among nations," one delegate to the Assembly intoned. The way forward had just been charted by the League itself in Austria and Hungary and by the recent acceptance of plans to resolve the long-standing reparations question.[36] The Genoa consensus lives. "Financial reconstruction is the basis of economic reconstruction."[37]

As for the specific goals of the conference, one of its principal supporters, the delegate from France, warned that it would not result in international treaties. Instead, "the Conference would enunciate a number of principles [and] it would seek some method of international cooperation to apply them." In consequence, in certain key sectors, it might bring about agreements among companies with the assent of governments that would ensure "stability of production and consumption."[38] In the background, quite evidently, were more or less organized business interests concerned about levels of protectionism rising since the end of the war.[39] "While separate national economies should be taken into consideration," members of the Assembly held, attention "should be directed toward the great natural lines of production which did not stop short at frontiers."[40]

Today the IMF often seeks to keep its focus on macroeconomic issues but finds itself interacting ever more intensively with its sister organizations. Similarly, in the course of preparing an agenda for the conference, League officials came to see that the issues of trade and cartels had to be much more prominent than issues of financial stabilization. They also came to see that an interstate consensus at a general level of principle was all that could be expected. As long as all principal powers joined in that consensus, however, such an outcome was viewed as contribution enough for one conference. As the minutes of the preparatory committee noted, "The Committee has borne in mind throughout, that the economic conference must be regarded not as an isolated event but as a stage in the continuous work of international collaboration in the economic sphere which had begun before the project of a general conference was launched and will continue when the conference itself is over."[41]

The International Economic Conference was finally held in Geneva in May 1927; 194 official delegates and 157 expert advisers attended. Forty-six member-states of the League were represented, as were the United States, the Soviet Union, and a few other non-members. A plethora of resolutions came out of the conference, all of them unanimous save for a few reservations. That unanimity, however, was purchased at the cost of specificity and in the absence of binding conviction. Two examples will suffice.

On the thorniest trade issue, the final resolutions reported agreement that the mutual grant of most-favored-nation (MFN) treatment on customs duties and other conditions of trade was "essential" to the expansion of international trade. Beyond a reference to the dangers of exchange-rate depreciation, the connection between MFN and stable finance was not the subject of much discussion. But clear in the background was the fact that major trading countries, led by Britain in 1925, had returned to a variant of the gold standard.

On the issue of industrial cartels, the conference unanimously recognized the benefits of "rationalization," which if "coordinated and far reaching" should result in a "better distribution of wealth." Of course, the extent to which "international industrial agreements" contributed to that rationalization could not be specified at the level of principle. National legislation should not necessarily be prejudiced against such "cartels," since they might indeed be "actuated by a sense of the general interest." Recognizing, however, that national approaches in fact differed quite strikingly, "effort toward international supervision seemed premature."[42]

Despite the striking similarity of these pronouncements to items now on the agenda not of the IMF but the WTO, what was to follow in international economic history gives such words a bitter aftertaste. To some extent, they had such a taste even then. One delegate to the conference noted that the resolutions provided nothing more than a "glimpse into the obvious."[43] But to others, the consensus achieved in Geneva was a more formidable achievement. On financial as well as trade issues, "a comprehensive code of policy behavior" had been agreed on.[44] Moreover, conference participants designated the League as the institution to flesh out that code and its implications. They even took steps to improve its "machinery" for joint discussion and problem-solving.

In practice, a beefed-up secretariat would be asked to build on the preparatory work of the conference. The statistical and analytical work that expanded throughout the final nineteen years of the League's life had its start here, and it constituted the institutional core of a recognizable precursor to the multilateral surveillance role of the IMF. Among other tasks, the machinery assisted the Financial Committee of the League in mandates deriving from the Geneva Conference to design new forms of financial assistance for troubled countries and to improve the functioning of the gold-exchange standard as it was evolving after 1925.

By 1927 it was clear that the fundamental nature of the economic oversight role of the League had already been defined, both through the results of conferences and through specific lessons learned during technical assistance missions. The League was to be a consensus-seeker. The underlying theory was one of natural policy convergence across interdependent member-states and modest reinforcement by a small group of League professionals. At most, the League would provide temporary buffers between members themselves and between them and the markets. And those markets—in goods, capital, even policies—would do the real work. As we shall see, the unanimity rule and what we might call the automaticity principle were fatal flaws, both of which the designers and staff of the IMF would eschew as they recovered and embellished the buffering role the League had pioneered.

Most of the practical tasks for the League coming out of the Geneva Conference focused directly on the external aspects of policy. But where serious domestic differences existed on such issues as the supervision of cartels, differences that might have clear external consequences, League oversight turned out to be quite reticent. And so it is all the more ironic that the global economic conflagration which began two years after the Geneva Conference found its spark in the one major area of policy on which the League had the least reticence and the longest history of principled oversight. Despite the apparently durable and practical consensus on first principles of "sound" finance, which dated back to Brussels in 1920, the catastrophe began in the financial markets.

The ultimate causes of the Great Depression continue to be much analyzed and much debated.[45] This is not the place to rehearse that debate. It is the place, however, to highlight an important correlation. When the economic recovery of the 1920s ended, the incipient surveillance machinery of the League became increasingly analytical and decreasingly practical. Encouraging constructive, problem-solving dialogue between competitive states is difficult at the best of times; the world was now entering the worst.

League staffers nevertheless perceived some momentum coming out of the Geneva Conference to create a mechanism that might facilitate a workable compromise between the restoration of a global "laissez-faire" economic system and the joint political management of the world "as an indivisible economic unit." As Per Jacobsson, who was then a member of the League's Secretariat and would later become a managing director of the IMF, put it:

> [The Geneva Conference] reached a synthesis of the two main economic ideas of the last century expressed on the one hand, by the Manchester School concentrating upon the advantages of free competition and, on the other hand, by manifold movements aiming at improvement in social conditions and insisting upon the rights of society as a whole.[46]

The synthesis soon unraveled not at the level of principle but at the level of practice. After major economies adopted a gold-exchange standard during the mid-1920s, many had few alternatives to contracting their domestic economies in the face of widening imbalances in external payments. Business investment, the fuel for economic prosperity, required efficient capital markets, and both required confidence. Confidence required sound money. And sound money appeared to require both the anchor of gold convertibility at fixed exchange rates and balanced budgets. The unfortunate consequences of policies based on such principles—unemployment and illiquidity—would, statesmen, League officials, and leading economists all hoped, heal themselves. The legitimacy problem posed by the fact that domestic political necessities and international economic principles were in fundamental conflict would go away if it was ignored. All that was needed was time and intestinal fortitude.

Inside the League, agreement on basic principles remained unquestioned until idiosyncratic voices from outside began calling for reconsideration. In hindsight, it might seem that unemployment, which in the United States had gone from 3 percent in 1929 to 25 percent in 1933, with comparable levels reached in Europe, created a climate for radical policy change. But the theoretical case for alternative policies had not yet been made, and the real architects of the coming policy revolution, Adolf Hitler and Franklin Roosevelt, were just coming to power. As the last of the great international economic conferences before World War II, the London Conference of 1933, would show, the case for orthodoxy remained intact.

CHAPTER 4

The Transformation of Economic Oversight in the League

O UTSIDE THE AUSPICES OF THE LEAGUE, THE FAMOUS DAWES AND Young plans, which channeled financial flows from the United States to Germany, rekindled broader international lending activity by the late 1920s. The conventional wisdom at the time held that the twin issues of reparations and inter-allied debt repayments were thereby being resolved. The financial collapse of 1929–31, however, brought those issues squarely back to the agenda. The League and its incipient systemic oversight capabilities would be rediscovered and transformed in directions no one had anticipated, but not before an event that would do much to discredit the organization as a whole.

The World Economic Conference of 1933

In 1932, representatives of the major governments involved met in Lausanne to negotiate final settlement of war debts. On the theory that it was better to do late than never what obviously needed to be done, they decided to cancel remaining reparations payments entirely. Doing so, they realized, amounted to throwing a small pebble into a stormy sea. But what was to be done about the tidal wave then coursing through the international economy? Why, of course, call for another conference and give it a broader mandate. And that is what they did. Thus was born the ill-starred World Economic Conference of 1933.

League officials tried later to distance themselves from what many thought would become a debacle. Although no League committee or member of the Secretariat recommended the conference, it was technically convoked by a resolution of the League's Council. Moreover, the EFO worked closely with the preparatory committee of experts appointed by Germany, Belgium, France, Great Britain, Italy, and Japan. The resulting agenda included a detailed program of action. As the program demonstrated, the orthodox economic principles established at Brussels and Genoa remained intact.

On monetary issues, the program was based on a major report prepared in 1932 by the Financial Committee of the League—with one striking exception.[1] At its core, the program called for a restoration of the gold-exchange standard, which Britain had once again abandoned in 1931 in the wake of a massive speculative attack on the pound sterling.[2] To ensure that countries had adequate gold reserves for such a restoration, the program specified that intergovernmental debts must be settled and free international movement of "goods, services, and capital" must be attained. The program advocated, therefore, that budgets be balanced but allowed that a stimulus could be provided to business by loosening internal monetary policies and reflating to achieve a new equilibrium.

The program called for countries still on the gold-exchange standard to allow for the free outward flow of gold and other forms of capital. Countries not on the standard, however, should not seek commercial advantage by depreciating the external value of their currencies below the point necessary to reestablish internal equilibrium. Despite the experience of 1931 and the 1932 League report finding that controls on "unproductive" capital flows might sometimes be justified, the program bluntly urged the abolition of all exchange controls.[3] Central banks, moreover, should be "independent" and freed from "political interference." They should also be encouraged to maintain "close and continuous" cooperation with one another. On the trade front, the program recommended that tariffs should first be frozen at existing levels, and then reduced through unilateral, bilateral, and group measures under a multilateral umbrella. Once "normal conditions" returned, unconditional MFN status should form the basis of international commercial relations. Finally, national economies should be more "flexible."[4]

The bankers had obviously gotten to the politicians in the run-up to the 1933 conference. In light of developments then transpiring inside major economies, the blind faith of the conference program in market solutions is truly breathtaking. Not surprisingly, therefore, the conference left unspecified the role it foresaw for actual multi-lateral institutions in either the financial or the economic field. The consequence of that silence, reinforced by the subdued role of the League Secretariat in the preparations for conference itself, seems clear. League oversight function would be limited to clarifying the rationale for policies based on enlightened self-interest. Rightly conceived at the level of principle, national policies aimed at restoring a functioning gold-exchange standard without capital controls and at creating a transparent and free trading system would automatically achieve optimal internal and external equilibria. Dilemmas of political legitimacy in an integrating international economy would yield to rhetorical solutions. Impeccable ideas rule, once they are explained clearly enough!

In fact, actual government policies were with few exceptions moving in precisely the opposite direction. The basic problem was not that conditions had become inauspicious for collective action along the lines specified by established principles. It was that those principles seemed discredited by experience even as the London Conference was called to order. The most "flexible" national economy was then watching its banking system collapse. The "sound money" policies of the U.S. Federal Reserve were just then deepening a major liquidity crisis and sapping business confidence. In such an environment, the United States left the gold-exchange standard just before the conference opened. Shaped by orthodox fears of inflationary spirals, balanced budgets were accelerating deflation there and elsewhere. In Germany, orthodox fiscal policy had just helped snuff the life out of a comatose Weimar Republic. The constituency for liberal commercial policies was in full retreat around the world. Competitive currency depreciation had become commonplace.[5]

When the World Economic Conference finally convened in London in June 1933, the spokesmen for the sixty-six nations represented could not bring themselves to depart from orthodoxy. In the background, however, the cognitive dissonance created by the widening gap between economic theory and actual policy stimulated debate, both inside the Secretariat of the League and more broadly. The broader debate continues to this day, and it would be fruitless to attempt a summation here. Suffice it to note, however, that the orthodox position retained its intellectual respectability.

Friedrich von Hayek, the famous Austrian economist then at the London School of Economics, was certainly not alone in building an impressive edifice of theory, the major implication of which was that in the long run, market-interventionist policies typically did more harm than good. On precisely this point, albeit based on the conviction that deep depressions bred unusual circumstances, John Maynard Keynes and his allies picked up the cudgels. The theoretical revolution thereby sparked seems so clear to us now, but in 1933 the core ideas were not yet fully formulated or compelling. With no other lodestar than the principles of Brussels and Genoa to guide them, therefore, the delegates to the London Conference had no basis for recommending new departures in national economic policies. Imagine their consternation, then, when their collective appeal to the United States for leadership in restoring the gold-exchange standard after an orderly devaluation and realignment of exchange rates brought a blunt and personal rejection from President Roosevelt himself. For good measure, the president excoriated "the fetishes of so-called international bankers."[6]

In July 1933, the World Economic Conference dissolved in intellectual and political disarray. As Keynes wrote at the time, there was "no cat in the bag, no rabbits in the hat—no brains in the head." Its consequence was "miserable confusion and unutterable waste of opportunity" brought about by "an obstinate adherence to ancient rules of thumb." More tellingly and less self-servingly, Keynes concluded at the time that new rules of thumb or even common sense could promise no better outcome. They would matter only if "a single power or a like-minded group of powers" could forge a new and practical consensus on them.[7]

To Keynes as well as to a few of his contemporaries, the weak link in the system as it had evolved incrementally throughout the 1920s was finance. As noted, a quite robust consensus had emerged after the Armistice that private financial markets should be relied on to support economic reconstruction and expansion. The mobility of private capital internationally, stable exchange rates promised by a restored gold-exchange standard, and passive domestic economic policies seemed to form a coherent whole. In the circumstances of the 1920s, it was difficult to imagine an alternative and practicable combination. That the consequence of the consensus was a speculative financial boom ending in profound economic collapse becomes clear only in hindsight.

Financiers then as now repeat the mantra "sound money, sound policies" because they know their activities depend on stable expectations of value, of risk, and of repayment. After the unanimity of the 1927 conference, it seemed to almost everyone that a principled basis for stable expectations had been restored. But practice did not follow principle, and iconoclasts like Keynes were beginning to think that the problem lay in the principles themselves. The economic arm of the League, whose raison d'être rested on those principles, was caught up in the contradiction. As Salter recalled, with a characteristic and far-from-disinterested degree of overstatement:

> Everything which was begun [by the League] early enough to come to fruition in the twenties was successful; everything that could not reach this stage till the thirties failed. Thus the plans which the Financial Committee were considering after their earlier work had been completed (whether on financial assistance in a new form to other countries in difficulty or the victims of aggression or on reform of the gold standard), all came to nothing. Unhappily, the same fate . . . befell the major task

attempted by the economic section—the establishment of a better foundation of commercial policy for international trade.[8]

In the mid- to late 1930s, nevertheless, the ultimate futility of the League's work could only be sensed. All hopes were not yet dashed, and that work continued. As the terrible decade advanced, the operational side of the League's oversight role fell into desuetude. Its analytic face, however, came to the fore. This did not stop the depression or impede preparations for war, but the experience did shape the worldviews of certain key individuals who would in their own careers bridge the distance between the League and the Fund.

League Oversight during the Great Depression

Despite the sense of foreboding that enveloped the economic work of the League after 1933, a quite remarkable transformation began inside the organization. Ironically, however, the constructive consequences of that transformation became evident only after the League ceased to exist. Forged in the furnace of the 1930s, a new model, a new procedure, and a new pragmatism quietly reshaped the practice of multilateral economic oversight in the final decade of the League's existence. Forced by hard political facts to retreat from the more assertive role that its predecessors had assumed in the 1920s, a retreat reinforced by the political dynamics of international economic negotiations in the 1930s, the EFO became a central analytic apparatus for shaping a new policy consensus. In this respect, it became—by accident and not by design—a direct precursor to the contemporary IMF.

To be sure, less esoteric work continued at the League during the early and mid-1930s. The financial panic that swept Europe after 1931 devastated the countries whose external borrowing the League had supervised in the 1920s. Austria, Hungary, and others were quickly pushed from hard-won solvency back to the brink of default. When they appealed once more for League assistance, methods applied before were applied again. League representatives calmed international lenders, helped craft new syndicates (often under official guarantees from leading European governments), and directly supervised debt-servicing operations in borrowing countries. Once again, this most concrete manifestation of multilateral oversight, although of marginal importance when all of Europe was heading toward the abyss of total war, was a harbinger of things to come. Decades later the IMF would play a similar role.[9] But the abysmal failure of the London Conference could not help but affect the way the League approached all of its future economic and financial tasks.

The high-water mark for its earlier approach, in fact, had been reached in 1927. Throughout the 1920s the chief objective of the League was to frame international conventions "to facilitate economic and financial relations between nations and thus contribute towards fulfilling the economic obligations laid upon members of the League by the Covenant."[10] On the basis of "international legislation" at the level of principle, markets would work much as they had in the era before World War I. Only a few agreed rules were necessary, most important the rules of the gold-exchange standard and of nondiscriminatory trade. To the extent adjustments were required in other domestic policies or arrangements so as to facilitate peaceful international intercourse, they would occur automatically.

After 1933, such a stance became increasingly untenable. The League therefore adapted its oversight role in two ways. First, although it never attempted to convene another world economic conference, it did gather information, draft reports, and sponsor meetings on specific questions, such as the trade-depressing issue of double taxation. When such meetings occurred, however, it always limited attendees to those states most directly involved, and it often sought to promote bilateral "model" agreements that might over time become multilateralized.[11] Second, it devoted increasing attention to systemic analysis, much of which pointed to the need for governments and international agencies deliberately to encourage convergent domestic policies. In short, the deficiency of markets left to their own devices became a focal point for the League's analytic work.

Alexander Loveday, director of the EFO from 1931 until the end, likened the most obvious application of the latter method of operation to the establishment of special governmental commissions or inquiries, a method that remains quite common in parliamentary systems throughout the world.[12] Commissions can indeed be a useful tool of governance, sometimes to build a constituency for a specific policy change, sometimes to postpone change until such a constituency emerges. So it was in the 1930s, when the League created expert committees to address such matters as multilateral payment systems, exchange controls, restrictions on the sale of raw materials, and standards for international loan contracts.

The League's new approach built on the precedent of its first survey, compiled in 1922 at the behest of the Brussels Conference. As a method of systemic oversight, it seemed a natural outgrowth of the kinds of preparatory work the staff always did before major conferences. Data were collected by neutral observers, general patterns were identified, and recommendations were made. The real novelty of the approach lay in the framing of those recommendations in terms of the facts as League analysts perceived them rather than in terms of orthodox economic principles.

Within the Secretariat of the League, staff members had been gathering, analyzing, and publishing economic statistics as early as 1919. Over time, an Economic Intelligence Service was formally organized within the Economic, Financial, and Transit Department. By the 1930s, although still modest in scale, the Service had developed into a kind of internal think-tank. Aside from regular statistical publications—the direct ancestors of contemporary statistical series published by the IMF and other international economic agencies—the Service also published an annual volume entitled *World Economic Survey.* Largely written by prominent consultants to the League—J. B. Condliffe in the early 1930s and James Meade from 1938 to 1940—its descendant is the *World Economic Outlook* of the IMF, which the Fund describes today as a central element in the contemporary practice of multilateral economic surveillance.[13]

In addition to Condliffe and Meade, a remarkable group of economists came to be associated with the Economic Intelligence Service, either directly as staff members and overseers or indirectly as consultants. They included Gottfried Haberler, Alvin Hansen, Folke

Hilgerdt, Tjalling Koopmans, Ragnar Nurkse, Jan Tinbergen, J. M. Fleming, Jacques Polak, and Louis Rasminsky.[14] All would later influence the work of the IMF, and the last three would rise to prominence in the ranks of its senior staff and on its executive board.

In 1933, the Rockefeller Foundation began supplementing the resources devoted to the Service by the League. Driven by concern over the deepening consequences of the depression, the foundation's purpose in providing an annual grant of $125,000 was to stimulate a broad research program on the international transmission of business cycles.[15] Most notably, the grant helped support a seminal study by Haberler, first published by the League in 1937.[16] Tinbergen and Polak then completed a massive empirical study aimed at testing Haberler's central hypotheses. With the publication of Tinbergen's two-volume *Statistical Testing of Business Cycle Theories* and follow-up work by Koopmans, Meade and Nurkse, the Economic Intelligence Service pioneered the field of open-economy macroeconomics.[17] The theoretical and methodological underpinnings for multilateral economic surveillance as practiced today by the IMF and other international organizations may be traced back to that work. Clearly bridging the beginnings of the oversight role of the soon-to-be-born IMF and that earlier work were a set of original policy-oriented studies undertaken by the Service during the war.

As the political situation in Europe deteriorated and war seemed imminent, League officials sought to build on their analytic work by presenting governments with an accessible compilation of advice on countercyclical economic policies. The Special Delegation on Depressions was established and asked to undertake the task. The delegation actually comprised an eight-member subcommittee of the Economic and Financial committees of the League. Two members were appointed from each committee, one was seconded from the International Labour Organisation, and three outside experts were contracted—Oskar Morgenstern, Jacques Rueff, and Bertil Ohlin. The composition of the delegation changed somewhat during the war years. Throughout its work, however, it was assisted by Loveday and his staff, including Ragnar Nurkse, Jacques Polak, and Louis Rasminsky.[18] Three major publications resulted: *The Transition from*

War to Peace Economy; International Currency Experience; and *Economic Stability in the Post-War World.*[19]

The studies of the delegation were widely acknowledged as having a significant impact on policymaking, both during and after the war. They did not, of course, appear in a vacuum, and the intellectual consensus they articulated needs to be interpreted in the context of the gathering Keynesian revolution. Immediately after the war, moreover, they would be criticized for exaggerating the risk of a reversion to depression and for giving insufficient attention to the problem of latent inflation.[20] But a few themes bear underlining, for they more or less anticipated the mandates later assigned to a new set of international economic institutions established by the victorious powers.

The reports underlined the need for "progressive removal of obstructions to trade," for avoidance of competitive cycles of currency depreciation, for acknowledgment of the "international character of cyclical economic depressions," and for "courageous international measures of reconstruction and development."[21] But none of these goals, it was noted, could be reached in the absence of more intensive cooperation among states. Throughout the interwar period, this truism lay behind the oft-repeated appeal for states to pursue their "enlightened self-interest" by remolding their policies around the ideals of free trade and the gold standard. The novelty of the depression studies was to ground that appeal in negotiated codes of conduct that entailed deliberate efforts to render compatible those domestic policies which had external effects. Gone was the earlier faith in the efficacy of markets guided by vague commitments to nondiscriminatory trade and currency stability. Underneath a new sense of pragmatism lay incipient acknowledgment that the disjunction between national politics and international economics required management. The depression had thrown the legitimacy dilemma into sharp relief. Practical tools, not rhetorical principles, were needed.

Alexander Loveday, who directed the League's depression reports and personally contributed to the first, claimed to have come to just such a conclusion as early as 1937.[22] Moreover, if such codes were to be more than idealistic expressions of principle, like the League's major economic pronouncements ever since the Brussels Conference, Loveday asserted that they required monitors and arbiters with real authority. Such authority could be delegated only by states, and although states would never delegate as much as Loveday might have hoped, the surveillance mandate of the IMF and other postwar multilateral organizations was thereby anticipated.[23]

In a more direct way, the reports also pushed the incipient new consensus, which we now identify with Keynes's 1936 *The General Theory of Employment, Interest, and Money,* beyond the old free trade/gold standard mantra. As might have been expected in the midst of a war that pitted democratic systems of government against totalitarian ones, the report stressed the "liberty of each individual" to make basic economic choices. But such liberty could be meaningful and contribute to "rising standards of living" in all countries only when governments provided the necessary domestic conditions to ensure that "no man or woman able and willing to work should be unable to obtain employment for periods of time longer than is needed to transfer from one occupation to another or, when necessary, to acquire a new skill."[24] For the full employment policies thereby justified to work on a global basis without compromising the overarching goals of expanded trade and stable exchange rates, the ultimate conclusion of the earlier studies of Haberler and Tinbergen seemed unavoidable. Relevant *national* policies must be coordinated directly by states themselves, if necessary through intermediary agencies created by them for just such a purpose. No external constraint, no autonomous market, nothing beyond the exercise of their own political will could bring those policies to converge.

Significantly, the League's depression reports emphasized trade in "raw materials and manufactured goods," not international flows of capital. Even though Nurkse's *International Currency Experience* laid substantial blame for interwar economic disorder upon speculative capital flows, the reports did not embrace the principle of capital control. Indeed, capital flows were a vital component of the early world system models of Tinbergen and Polak, which lay in the background. In general, there was no bias in the studies against what would later be called "equilibrating capital flows." There was also no answer to the question how to differentiate such flows in practice from disequilibrating flows, a question that would later plague the Bretton Woods system. The reports simply presumed that financial flows to accommodate expanding trade would be important for the avoidance of depressions after the war, and they did not envisage the continuation of the extensive system of capital controls that had been built up during the war. Nevertheless, without being completely explicit, they clearly did envisage a postwar system that would give priority to trade and therefore to the stability of exchange rates, not to the mobility of capital. Especially in a context where governments would pursue activist employment policies while avoiding competitive currency depreciation and other "obstructions to trade," the freedom of capital movements, though desirable, would have to be conditional. Conditional on what? The League reports, once again, provided the answer: conditional on effective arrangements for interstate coordination of a full range of national economic policies having consequences for those exchange rates.

The final economic studies of the League would contribute to a new consensus that found its authoritative expression in the 1944 Bretton Woods Agreement on monetary and financial issues and in the 1947 Havana Charter on trade. Ultimately, those studies helped provide an intellectual basis for finally rejecting the agreed principles and the methods associated with the Brussels and Genoa conferences. In the terms introduced in earlier chapters, the old consensus rested on the ideal of free trade as well as on the objectives of exchange rate stability through a gold-exchange standard, neutral domestic economic policies keyed on balanced budgets, and capital mobility. The new consensus promoted "the progressive removal of obstructions to trade," "orderly" exchange-rate adjustment (either up or down as internal and external economic fundamentals warranted) through a transparent set of monitored arrangements, countercyclical fiscal and monetary policies, and capital mobility to the extent necessary to achieve these prior objectives.

The old policy consensus informed the two-dimensional, multilateral oversight function of the League: it provided principles for direct application in financially desperate countries, and it unified pioneering analytical surveys of the international economy. The new consensus shaped the surveillance functions of the international agencies that arose from the ashes of the League. As became clear over time, and especially in the IMF, those functions would now have three dimensions. The first two were similar in form to those of the League, but the principles behind them were less rigid and their application much more pragmatic; the third had to do with the nature of the intergovernmental codes of conduct crafted at the start of an era of activist economic policies. Where variants of the gold standard promised but rarely delivered the "automatic" adjustment of national economies to the pressures of openness, the structure of the IMF and its evolving surveillance function created space for judgment and political accommodation. Although this situation frustrated the Fund's staff in its early years—after all, they were mainly economists, and economists have always loved clear principles—a basic pragmatism lay at the very core of the Fund. The Fund was to be a buffer for states in between national programs of economic security and the exigencies of international markets. Those markets, in short, provided a means to an end. They were no longer ends in themselves.

The Legacy of the League

The League was well represented at the 1944 Bretton Woods Conference. Alexander Loveday attended as an official observer. Having left the organization in 1943, Jacques Polak was a member of the Dutch delegation. Louis Rasminsky, who also left in 1943 to become an official in the Canadian government, played a key role in brokering the main negotiations between the Americans and the British. Nevertheless, there exists very little evidence that the chief architects of the new system drew seriously or directly on the League's experience. Neither Polak nor Rasminsky recalls Loveday having any real impact on the proceedings.[25] Their own thinking was, of course, shaped by their years at the League, but both concede that the British, and especially the Americans, spent little time pondering what had gone before. The League-sponsored business cycle and depression studies were of course in the background, but so was Keynes' *General Theory*—and Keynes was there in person. Nevertheless, the bright lights of Keynes's ideas and America's power at Bretton Woods have blinded us to the enduring impact of the League on the IMF, at its founding and as it would evolve in later years.

As Martin Hill explained when the EFO was being closed down in 1945:

> The creation of the Organization represented an entirely new departure in peacetime interstate relationships. . . . Numerous multilateral agreements that would not have been possible without an appropriate international machinery were concluded. . . . Consultation between officials engaged in framing and executing economic and social policies in different countries was rare before 1914; through the League it became an established practice. Even more important perhaps was the remarkable change in general public attitudes toward international consideration of economic problems. . . . In 1920, national tariffs were generally held to be a matter of purely domestic concern. The same is true of many other problems, the international consideration of which is now just as generally considered to be normal and desirable.[26]

Similar things would be said about the IMF years later, but we need to ask whether such a view of the League, in retrospect, warrants our skepticism.

Certainly, the first permanent director of the EFO thought so when he published his memoirs in 1961. Despite its achievements, Lord Salter, like most commentators on the League since then, focused on the ultimate failure of the League, which he blamed on "the intrinsic weakness of an 'inter-state' institution: a deterioration in the relations between its principal members can quickly reduce it to impotence." To Salter, the League merely represented "organized diplomacy, not an organ of Government . . . [and] it is an illusion to believe that 'technical' work of real importance can continue successfully if there is a basic disunity in the controlling political authority."[27] The shock of war, more than any institutional creation of states, accounted for whatever cooperative impulses came to characterize the contemporary period.

But Salter's realism is more problematic than Hill's idealism. The kind of supranational institution conjured by the image of a unified "controlling political authority" is unimaginable in any world with an international political structure resembling our own. Equally unimaginable is the autonomous work of "technical" organizations in such a context. The history surveyed above supports a more complex view of the League and its legacy.

The economic work of the League was not irrelevant to the post-World War II era, nor was it forgotten. In a number of important respects the experience foreshadowed what was to come. Moreover, lessons learned during the life of the League were transmitted directly into at least one of its most important postwar analogs.

In the 1920s, the restoration of a world economy on the foundation of global financial markets seemed to require a basic form of collaboration among states. In institutional terms, they needed a buffer. The League's halting and often frustrating engagement in the incipient practice of systemic oversight evolved in such an environment. In its directly applied form, that is, in response to Central European debt crises, that role was straightforward. States principally needed an institution to blame for anticipated failure, but they also welcomed the slight chance that the coordinating function provided by that institution could avoid failure. In its more analytic form, and in an age of conference diplomacy, League oversight gave states an instrument to compile reliable data across different national settings, diagnose trends, and suggest directions for mutually beneficial policy adjustments.

Both forms of oversight were practiced in the 1920s, and both relied on a fairly general consensus among League members on economic principles that applied equally to all of them. By the late 1920s, following conference after conference, such a consensus existed. In fact, the principles of the gold standard, fiscal conservatism, capital mobility, and nondiscriminatory trade, as well as the belief that any necessary policy adjustments would come automatically once agreement on such principles had been reached, had become an ideology—useful for keeping capital flowing, at least for a time, but increasingly out of step with the real world inside national political economies. The principled consensus turned out to be theoretical at best and illusory at worst.

The 1930s transformed the oversight role of the League and privileged its analytic face.[28] The economic catastrophe of that decade also overthrew the earlier dominant ideology and dramatically promoted the virtues of pragmatism. It did not, however, subvert the idea that a multilateral buffer was needed if a world of decentralized political authority was to return to the path of economic and financial integration. As in the 1920s, the buffer was there for crisis management tasks as well as for scapegoating in the event of disaster, but its analytic role was different. The League would still compile and assess cross-national data, it would still organize conferences, albeit more focused and less ambitious ones, and it would still make suggestions for sound national policies. But its overarching goal was to facilitate deliberate policy coordination, a feasible mechanism for managing a legitimacy problem that would never go away in a world of independent states with interdependent economies. In a world chary of economic rules that no political power could render binding, in other words, the League in its last days tried to provide a rationale for discretionary national policies to move in internationally constructive directions.

The ambition behind such systemic oversight, and the hard experience that shaped it, was transmitted from a dying League to a rising IMF. The negotiations at Bretton Woods, and even more clearly those at Savannah in 1946 which activated the IMF, put an end to the dream of automaticity, at least for a time. National policies having external economic effects would have to be supervised and adjusted, if necessary through political coordination encouraged through the workings of a system of pegged exchange rates facilitated by a credible and neutral intermediary. Over time, as the exchange-rate system became even more discretionary, the need for a broader kind of policy coordination intensified and the mandate of the intermediary became more expansive.

The next chapter shows how, after a rocky start, the new intermediary did gain more credibility, more substance, and more influence than the League ever had, even in its heyday. In this respect, the negative lessons of the League's experience were learned. In a few short decades, however, the dream of automaticity returned. With the restoration of international capital markets on a scale that approached the ambitions of the League's overseers in the 1920s, the new intermediary found itself playing far different roles than its own founders originally intended. Its core mandate came to resemble the one pioneered by the League.

CHAPTER 5

Global Aspirations and the Early International Monetary Fund

*T*HE SURVEILLANCE FUNCTION OF THE INTERNATIONAL MONETARY Fund has existed in embryonic form ever since the organization was established. The term itself did not gain general currency until the 1970s, however, when the function was grounded in legal obligations applicable to all Fund members. In a very basic sense, the acceptance of those obligations, implicitly in 1944 and explicitly three decades later, was a response to the depression studies of the League of Nations. Indeed, the painful era that the League itself had come to symbolize lay just below the surface when states gave those obligations an institutional expression by taking the constitutive decisions to shape and reshape the Fund's core mandate. At base, that mandate seemed the best practical means available to ameliorate a rising tension between the exigencies of national politics and the logic of global finance.

A substantial and complex literature now surrounds the general history of the Fund and what we now call its surveillance mandate. This chapter and the next do not aspire to provide a thorough synthesis. Instead, they trace principal threads of normative debate and institutional experimentation running through that history and connecting back to the experience of the League. This chapter examines the development of the Fund's responsibility for systemic oversight during the organization's early years; the next concentrates on the explication and transformation of such a mandate after the 1970s. The story tells us a great deal about the political foundations of the contemporary world economy, marked as it is by the kind of cross-border financial integration to which the founders of the League once aspired.

The Normative and Policy Context of Bretton Woods

The evolution of the surveillance function of the Fund needs to be viewed against the broader normative consensus that arose from the ashes of World War II, a consensus most clearly expressed in the 1944 Bretton Woods agreement. As noted in Chapter 2, the agreement sought in principle to reconcile increasingly liberal external economic relations with the retention by individual states of their right to intervene in their internal economies. Grounded in the basic liberal premise that expanding international trade held the key to stable economic reconstruction and development, the agreement aimed to create a set of supportive monetary arrangements. The common understanding was that the durability of those arrangements depended on adept management of economic adjustment, the scope of which was regularly quantified and summarized in national balance-of-payments accounts.

The adjustment problem is the practical face of the dilemma of political legitimacy in a world of independent states that collectively aspire to integrate their national markets more deeply. One way or another, the problem had to be faced directly after the war. In short, realistic mechanisms were needed to facilitate national economic adjustments that would not disrupt the restoration and progressive liberalization of international trade and investment. Where the League had failed, the founders of the IMF would try again.

At the heart of the original Bretton Woods design were open current accounts and fixed but adjustable exchange rates supervised by a multilateral arbiter. With a degree of hyperbole, Fund documents liked to refer to this as a "regulatory" role. In essence, states acceding to the Articles of Agreement provided the Fund with a threefold mandate: to monitor and discourage restrictions on current payments; to provide short-term financing to ease the adjustment of imbalances; and to oversee orderly changes in exchange rates in cases of "fundamental" payments disequilibria. To enable such a mandate to be fulfilled, signatory states agreed to "collaborate with the Fund to promote exchange stability, to maintain orderly exchange arrangements, and to avoid competitive exchange alterations."[1]

In institutional terms, this commitment initially entailed participation by members not yet prepared to accept the full obligations of the Bretton Woods "par value" exchange-rate system in the "consultations" process of the Fund. Practically speaking, it applied mainly to those members not prepared to allow their currencies to be freely convertible into other currencies and into gold at set prices. Eventually, that legal commitment expanded to include all member-states, whether they had inconvertible currencies or not. The consultations process therefore came to constitute the practical core of what would become the Fund's surveillance function.

Although accepting an obligation to collaborate is hardly as substantive as, say, establishing a common currency, an irrevocably fixed exchange rate, or a joint central bank, the historical record indicates that the member-states of the Fund have rarely taken that obligation lightly or treated it as inconsequential. Moreover, since it was from the start tied in with an explicit effort to encourage member-states to move toward currency convertibility, it was a key element in a fresh attempt to restore a world wherein capital would be readily movable across national borders. In this sense, and in terms of the policy trade-offs outlined in Chapter 2, the Bretton Woods agreement grappled with issues similar to those confronting the League in its early days.

The historiography on the 1944 agreement is extensive and detailed, as is the jurisprudential literature on its elaboration.[2] For present purposes, it is sufficient to focus on what that literature tells us about the motivations of those individuals who had the greatest impact on the negotiation and subsequent ratification of the final agreement.

The Bretton Woods Agreement

The final outcome of the Bretton Woods negotiations, and the initial agenda of the IMF, was a basic compromise between perceptions of the expected postwar interests of Britain and the United States in an environment widely forecast to be deflationary.[3] For his part, the head of the British delegation, John Maynard Keynes, anticipated a pressing need for external financing after the war but also a deep aversion in Parliament to external interference in the stimulative policies needed to restore domestic economic growth. Harry White, conversely, focused mainly on pressures directly reflected in the U.S. Congress to open foreign markets for American exports, to end preferential trading arrangements—such as those which prevailed among Britain, its colonies, and dominions—and to limit enduring external financial commitments. Linking the two chief negotiators, and biasing them toward some kind of agreement, was their mutual fear of a reversion to 1930s-style monetary policies after the war. Canadian official Louis Rasminsky, who had experienced the consequences of those policies during his fourteen-year career at the League, played an important role in bringing together their respective negotiating positions.[4]

Keynes's opening position gave central emphasis to monetary arrangements organized around rigidly fixed exchange rates, but he began in 1943 to push proposals for greater exchange-rate flexibility which rendered it easier for states to transfer the burden of economic adjustment away from internal markets and toward the external sector, thus giving vent to potential pressures for protectionism. In this regard, he anticipated the leftward tack of governance in Britain and elsewhere after the war.

For his part, White originally promoted the idea that an international referee should be able to require changes in the internal policies of member-states but later retreated when it met implacable British resistance. To simplify what was actually a complex bargain, in the end White reluctantly agreed to a system that in effect permitted large adjustments in the declared "par values" of exchange rates, but only under what were expected to be exceptional circumstances and only when the referee concurred. The plan also permitted the referee to express views to members on issues related to exchange arrangements. White agreed, however, that the referee was not to object to an exchange rate change considered necessary to deal with a "fundamental disequilibrium" or justified in light of "domestic social and political policies."[5] During the subsequent battles over confirmation of the Bretton Woods agreement, it became clear that neither negotiator had underestimated the depth of his political masters' concern about his handiwork.

Keynes faced the broadest possible antipathy to the agreement in the parliamentary debate that preceded British assent. As a U.S. Embassy official put it at the time, "The outstanding psychology of the debate seemed to be, first, that a post-war slump in the United States is inevitable and second, the fear that the United States does not allow Britain and other countries to adopt the necessary measures of self-defense and that, consequently, the United States will drag the whole world down with her into the abyss."[6] Although there existed a widespread sense that "self-defense" had proved self-defeating in the interwar years, the oversight role assigned to the Fund aroused particularly acute sensitivities. Since many parliamentarians suspected that this role would in effect provide a means for the United States to insist on domestic policy changes, Keynes himself took special pains to minimize its intended scope. Emphasizing the variability of exchange rates in the proposed system and the automaticity of borrowing rights, he even went so far as to assert that those policies would be "immune from criticism by the Fund."[7]

White confronted different concerns in Congress during the American ratification debate, and he emphasized quite different interpretations. Although somewhat wary of one provision of the agreement (the "scarce currency" clause) that could under certain circumstances allow countries to restrict U.S. dollar payments, and therefore to discriminate against imports from the United States, many legislators were more concerned that financing provided by the Fund might come with no conditions attached. In subsequent hearings, White and other administration spokesmen traversed a fine line. They sought to reassure their critics that "conditionality" would develop in practice and that Fund-promoted policies abroad would ensure that the United States was not held responsible for any future shortage of dollars. They also opened the door for private American banks and corporations to allay such a shortage by developing their international activities.

Despite doubts in some circles, ratification occurred on both sides of the Atlantic. Economic prostration surely tipped the balance in Britain, but the safeguards embedded in the final compromise helped. The liberal internationalist vision at the center of the IMF still raised profound challenges both for the British economy and for the component parts of an empire caught in a complex web of financial commitments.[8] But those challenges were ultimately eclipsed by the prospect of severe economic dislocation if renewed depression and American isolation followed the war. Nonetheless, a substantial body of opposition, both from the nationalist left and the traditionalist right, fought the agreement, and promoted alternative plans until the bitter end. Final assent was contingent on the Americans going first.

American opinion eventually swung decisively behind that vision in the anti-isolationist euphoria that greeted the termination of the war. In the end, the administration relied heavily on the argument that the Bretton Woods proposals represented the same opportunity to ensure world peace that the League of Nations had offered in 1921. Having missed the earlier chance, at such dreadful human and financial cost in the 1930s and 1940s, the United States could not afford to miss this second chance. "However exaggerated these arguments may seem in retrospect," recounts a close observer of the ratification debate, "they paid rich dividends at the time. . . . This feeling that 'we must take a chance'—that however imperfect, the Bretton Woods institutions must be tried—played a decisive role in winning final approval."[9] Casting the decision in terms of the seeming certainty of future losses proved crucial to winning approval for the overall agreement.[10]

From the start, however, the scope of the Bretton Woods agreement was limited by safeguards responsive to concerns about another kind of loss—the loss of domestic political authority occasioned by the working out of liberal internationalism in practice. The League had faced exactly the same conundrum in its day, but the outcome now was different. When the agreement was ratified, the 1930s were not at all distant in time and the memory of the League and its limitations still fresh. In retrospect, the step taken by states after World War II seems modest to those who emphasize, with considerable justification, that it did not create a supranational seat of political authority beyond the nation-state. But against the backdrop of the constitutional weakness of the League, and of broadly shared perceptions of the legacy of that weakness, the Bretton Woods agreement was indeed significant. It began a political process that would culminate in a clear breach of the formerly sacrosanct right of sovereign states to craft their economic policies without external accountability. Into that breach would march battalions of international public servants whose now codified mandate was to help states cope with the fact that the integrated markets to which they aspired could never be permanently grounded in the solid political foundations of their national markets.

American leaders clearly saw in the agreement a means of legitimating U.S. power in the postwar system.[11] As we shall see, however, that was only one part of a much more subtle process, in the years following Bretton Woods, more broadly to render politically legitimate the partial delegation of effective authority to international markets, especially financial markets. That delegation was surely compatible with the dominant domestic coalition constructed in the United States during the Bretton Woods ratification struggle, as well as with the general structure of its domestic governing arrangements in the postwar period. The bankers were not in charge, but no political coalition would emerge to oppose their evident interests in the decades following the implementation of the Bretton Woods agreement. Over time, many other states confronted a similar set of circumstances as they and their constituents sought the benefits of deepening involvement in external markets.

In the first instance, the specific oversight role assigned to the IMF in its early years reflected a widely shared and straightforward desire on the part of the United States and its allies to avoid a reversion to monetary anarchy. The analogy of the interwar period helped build a supportive political coalition in the key states by making the potential costs of noncooperation appear more certain; and a rather loose consensus on the limits of cooperation sealed the final agreement. As the oversight principle was later implemented, neither the United States nor Britain found itself entirely satisfied. But an innovative institutional structure had been put in place, with the potential for encouraging cooperative monetary behavior.

Note that other outcomes were possible; there was nothing inevitable about the Bretton Woods agreement or its ratification. Had the decision to accede been framed simply in terms of the economic gains that could accrue from cross-national policy collaboration, for example, it seems doubtful that a supportive coalition could have been structured either in Britain or in the United States. British policymakers had little interest in moving quickly to nondiscriminatory arrangements in money or trade; bailing out the world from the bankruptcy of the war years in order to achieve such gains held little attraction on Capitol Hill. Conversely, had U.S. policymakers framed the decision in terms of an unambiguous need to secure political gains now and in the future, say, by minimizing the safeguards that allowed other countries room for maneuver, it seems evident that the agreement would have foundered in Britain. In short, the way in which the decision was framed may plausibly be seen as making a difference. Economic openness, external accountability, and democracy fit awkwardly together. The interwar analogy and the memory of the League proved extremely useful in encouraging their tentative new embrace.

The Inception of Fund Oversight

In its first years, the oversight function of the Fund was associated most directly with those member-states availing themselves of Article XIV of the IMF Agreement, which permitted them to retain, during the "post-war transitional period," restrictions on payments and transfers for current international transactions.[12] On the assumption that transition would be a temporary phase, and to encourage members to embrace as quickly as possible the full obligations of Article VIII, that is, complete freedom of current payments and transfers, Article XIV required members maintaining exchange restrictions to consult regularly with the Fund.[13] The specific form of such consultations was actually presaged during the Bretton Woods negotiations.

Focusing on the expected length of time required to return to "normal" economic relations in the wake of the war, Keynes sought to preserve maximum flexibility for Britain to decide for itself when that point had been achieved. White originally sought to limit the transition to an explicit three years in order to limit the risk that postwar protectionism and discriminatory payment arrangements would become permanent. One British participant in the final negotiating session reported that White "tried hard to persuade us to abandon the idea of an indeterminate transitional period [and] Keynes threatened to walk out if he is pressed . . . on this matter."[14]

According to the official history of the Fund, the report of the American delegation on this particular meeting was less dramatic, but it made clear that strong views were expressed. Keynes was asked if "the British recognized that in joining the Fund they were accepting some obligations to modify their domestic policy in light of its international effects on stability"; he replied that they did but at their own discretion. "He finally seemed to admit," the minutes went on, "that it might be helpful to have an obligation to the Fund to back up those who were working for some modification of domestic policy, providing the Fund did not issue orders on some specific phase of domestic policy such as wages."[15] The final compromise, codified in Article XIV, provided that the Fund would begin to report internally on members' exchange restrictions three years after the start-up of operations and would begin to consult directly with such members after five years.

Significantly, Article XIV left the outer time limits of the transitional period undefined.[16] It is fair to say, however, that most participants and observers at the time thought the period would be reasonably short. They were mistaken. The practical difficulties involved both in removing restrictions under Article XIV and in accepting the full obligations of Article VIII were generally underestimated, especially for developing states. Britain itself, and most of its Continental neighbors, accepted Article VIII obligations only in 1958, when they were ready to make their currencies fully convertible once again. Even by the early 1990s, only half of the Fund's membership had successfully made the transition.[17] Article XIV consultations therefore assumed an importance and extent unanticipated at the beginning.

Before the actual start of the first round of consultations in the late 1940s, deep divisions were still present in the Fund's Executive Board. Consistent with its strategy at Bretton Woods and explicitly aiming to create a nondiscriminatory international economic regime, the United States obviously saw those consultations as a mechanism for pressuring states that maintained exchange restrictions, which often translated into restraints on dollar-based imports. Holding a different view on the necessity of such restrictions, the states to be consulted did not welcome the attention. Indeed, the cleavage lines demarcated in struggles over the breadth of Fund authority and the juridical status of its advice continually reappeared during the Fund's early years, with the United States and Canada frequently trying to widen interpretation of the Fund's mandate under Article XIV and Britain, Australia, India, and others fighting for a narrower interpretation.[18]

The most significant of the early debates inside the Fund concerned the extent of the consultation mandate.[19] Members subject to obligatory consultations wanted to circumscribe the Fund's scope and allow it to comment only on the financial aspects of particular exchange restrictions, but the United States pushed for broader Fund authority to inquire into the underlying factors that necessitated their retention. On an important procedural point, the Americans also fought to ensure that consultations resulted in the Executive Board taking a formal position on issues raised therein. In explicit board votes, the United States, which controlled some 30 percent of the total voting power, got its way on both counts. The bitterness left in the wake of these and other votes, however, quickly led the Americans to back off from their hard-line stance and the Fund's staff to couch the written conclusions of specific consultations in extremely cautious, deferential language. After these early debates, moreover, formal votes at board level on such questions became rare and decision making by consensus the norm.

The debates never succeeded in clarifying the definition of exchange restrictions. The Executive Board was therefore subsequently unable to draw a clear boundary between legitimate financial restraints and illegitimate trade impediments. Through interpretations actually articulated, definitions left unstated, and the subsequent tacit consensus on the need to limit board votes on sensitive policy matters, constraints on the Fund's formal authority over international capital movements implied in the articles gradually became established in practice.

The extent of the Fund's authority was also at the center of associated debates in its early years regarding conditions applicable when members sought to use its financial resources. A long and complicated discussion in the board finally led to a decision in October 1952 permitting the Fund to negotiate "stand-by" arrangements with members, arrangements that later provided increasing volumes of balance-of-payments financing to individual members subject to progressively stiffening requirements for changes in national economic policies.[20] Similar to the position of the League with respect to Austria and Hungary in the 1920s, such arrangements obviously expanded the potential influence of the Fund. But its formal right to attempt to influence Article XIV members through regular consultations was the same, whether those members required financing or not.

Few members would ever publicly express enthusiasm for the intervention of the Fund in their internal affairs, however circumscribed it might be in practice. The reason is obvious, especially for members with democratic systems of government. How could elected leaders ever explain to constituents that their own governments, by joining the Fund, had given outsiders—appointed international officials, no less—the formal, legal right to question sovereign national choices? Despite the problem, the handling of which has always been facilitated by the arcane subject matter of the Fund's mandate and, as we shall see, by its ultimate limitations, an ever-wider array of members came to appreciate the usefulness of Fund oversight throughout the 1950s. The mechanics of the consultations process were refined, and Fund economists gradually built a base of knowledge that they could bring to bear in helping members resolve specific adjustment problems. The venue of consultations also shifted throughout the decade. Initially the local representatives of member-states attended at the Fund's Washington headquarters; later, staff missions were sent out from Washington to the national capitals. Not least, this shift allowed Fund staff to consult with higher levels of national policy-makers and to improve the quality of their reports to the board.

In 1960 the members agreed on the necessity and appropriateness of the Fund collecting data on restrictive trade practices adopted for balance-of-payments purposes, a subject of acute sensitivity only a decade earlier. When the United States now pushed for a broadening of the Fund's ability to discourage the maintenance of exchange restrictions by individual members, consensus was readily achieved. The improved economic prospects of weaker member-states were obviously involved. But by 1960 it was also true that the effective limits of the Fund's powers were clearer. The Fund could encourage economic liberalization, but even when its financial resources were in play it could not force unwanted policy changes. It could, however, play the role of scapegoat for policy changes desired by leaders but resisted by their constituents.

Such a realization was undoubtedly in the background when the board later agreed to the inclusion in consultations of analysis of general fiscal and monetary policies, as well as other domestic policies having a direct or indirect impact on exchange rates and international payments balances. As the Fund's historian put it, "Agreement was eased by the understanding that no general precedents were being set . . . and that comments from the Fund might be helpful to the authorities of some countries in putting through politically unpopular policies."[21] Although the Fund later came to see such a role as a double-edged sword, as we shall see, it continues to play this and more subtle buffering roles.

Toward Symmetry in Principle

All things considered, the actual practice of Fund oversight by the 1960s had alleviated earlier fears that its expansion could come only at the expense of national political authority. The dual standard inherent in its application, however, continued to be a source of annoyance. Fund oversight soon became more "symmetrical" when the United States agreed to establish a precedent for voluntary consultations under Article VIII, a move unanticipated in 1944.

The move toward symmetry in the application of Fund procedures did not develop out of any sense of justice and equity on the part of its major promoter, the United States. The international monetary environment had changed. Since the war, the dollar had been the world's key currency, the central vehicle for facilitating international exchange. The architects at Bretton Woods aspired to re-create a workable gold-exchange standard through a system of stable but adjustable exchange rates. In truth, they had created the conditions for the natural growth of a dollar standard with less than smoothly adjusting exchange rates. During the early years, its flaw was a shortage of sufficient liquidity to quicken the pace of international reconstruction and growth. The symptom was a global shortage of dollars. When in the 1960s the member-states of the Fund finally began to address the problem seriously, by designing new instruments to augment the supply of international liquidity, they soon found themselves in a changed environment. That shortage of dollars was becoming a glut. In a system designed to promote equilibrium in national current accounts over the long run, the emerging dollar glut was the mirror image of entrenched American trade deficits.

As the 1960s opened, the United States began to confront its own international adjustment problem, a problem for which it required the ever more intensive collaboration of its trading and investing partners. In such a context, it promoted the idea that the Fund should begin regular annual consultations with Article VIII members, that is, with members like the United States which had fully convertible currencies. Such consultations, the Fund's Executive Board declared in its implementing decision, would enable the organization "to provide technical facilities and advice . . . or as a means of exchanging views on monetary and financial developments."²² But the fundamental reasons for, and constraints on, the consequent expansion of the Fund's role in this area are implicit in the declassified minutes of the first Article VIII consultation, which took place with the United States on March 5, 1962.²³

The consultation began with a meeting between the Fund's managing director, Per Jacobsson, and the interdepartmental National Advisory Council on International Monetary and Financial Problems, the high-level coordinating group created by Congress when it ratified the Bretton Woods Agreement. Jacobsson's opening remarks explicitly recalled the earlier consultations process initiated in the 1920s by the Financial Committee of the League of Nations, a process in which he had personally been involved as a young League staffer. Tactfully decrying the restricted nature of those consultations, limited to those countries in need of stabilization programs and rejected even by a few countries that fell into that category, Jacobsson hoped to send a message. Emphasizing the Bretton Woods notion that the international community had a *right* to voice opinions about national policies that had systemic implications, he stated, "Naturally, the attitude of the United States is in this, as in other matters, of the greatest importance since what the United States does becomes respectable for any other country."²⁴

Jacobsson went on in a subtle and diplomatic way to express concerns about, among other things, wage inflation in the United States that threatened to exacerbate international payments imbalances. In this vein, he opened the door to a discussion of problematic trends in U.S. fiscal and monetary policies. The American officials followed with detailed explanations and generally sought to demonstrate the complexities of the economic challenges then confronting them. Jacobsson concluded the meeting by observing "how varied the problems being faced by the U.S. were . . . [and that] the problems were well in hand."²⁵ Although later events would make his final judgment seem wildly optimistic, Jacobsson did reawaken the memory of the interwar period, and he found a receptive audience.

The Americans shared part of Jacobsson's agenda. The international outcome to be avoided was an irreconcilable dispute over how adjustment burdens should be distributed between national economies in external deficit and those in surplus. Voluntary Fund consultations under Article VIII and a continuation of required consultations under Article XIV just might help reduce the prospect of repeating a sad history. But Jacobsson's interlocutors did not share his concern about precisely how the reverberations of American policy decisions were then being transmitted through the international economy. A spokesman for the norms of Bretton Woods, Jacobsson believed that pegged exchange rates and objective oversight could help move even the United States itself toward what he called "sound" policies. But the earth was shifting under his feet.

A New Era Dawns

During the discussions leading up to the Bretton Woods agreement, a key sticking point between the principal negotiators had involved the issue of official controls on short-term capital movements in a system of pegged exchange rates. Although Keynes had moved away from his earlier view that finance was not one of those "things which should by their nature be international," he continued to believe strongly in the right of the state to impose capital controls as and when it perceived the need to arise.[26] White approached the matter differently. Although willing to concede that "disequilibrating" capital flows were both conceivable and undesirable, White envisaged a monetary order that would actively discourage all types of financial restrictions that impede trade and the international flow of "productive" capital.[27] The word "productive" here was carefully chosen; it was generally understood to distinguish such flows from "speculative" flows.

The American position obviously reflected the expectation that, as the major creditor in the postwar order, the United States stood to benefit from as liberal an environment for international investment as could be created. By the same token, however, the Americans were also intent on ensuring that access to the financial resources of the new international monetary institution they favored creating, the IMF, would be limited to countries facing short-term balance-of-payments problems; in the face of undesired capital outflows, the Americans preferred that a government undertake "adjustment" (in its exchange rate and/or the domestic policies producing its payments problem) rather than seek financing from other governments. They therefore contemplated a kind of regulatory mission for the IMF.

The final Bretton Woods compromise affirmed the priority of adjustment in the event of sustained capital outflows but, as noted, left the option of controls to the discretion of individual states, provided only that such controls were not intended to restrict trade.[28] For his part, Keynes interpreted this compromise as follows:

> Not merely as a feature of the transition, but as a permanent arrangement, the plan accords to every member Government the explicit right to control all capital movements. What used to be heresy is now endorsed as orthodox. . . . It follows that our right to control the domestic capital market is secured on firmer foundations than ever before, and is formally accepted as a proper part of agreed international arrangements.[29]

In the day-to-day experience of the IMF, the difficulty of making clear distinctions between illegitimate "exchange" restrictions and legitimate capital controls soon became apparent.[30] Among the leading industrial states, however, tensions related to such difficulties gradually ebbed after the restoration of currency convertibility in Europe in 1958 and in Japan in 1963. Indeed, when the dollar glut started to become clear shortly thereafter, the problem quickly turned on its head. The issue now was how to save the pegged exchange rate system when currencies were too readily convertible.

On December 12, 1961, the Council of the Organization for Economic Cooperation and Development (OECD) adopted the Code of Liberalization of Capital Movements in which the member-states agreed to "progressively abolish between one another" restrictions on movements of capital "to the extent necessary for effective economic cooperation."[31] Although the code represented the most explicit international statement of intent regarding capital controls, it left significant scope for member states to make exceptions for certain types of capital transfers and to take any actions considered necessary for the "maintenance of public order or . . . the protection of essential security interests."[32] In the event of balance-of-payments problems that it considered severe, a member-state was also permitted by the code "temporarily" to derogate from its liberalization obligations.[33] At the very least, it could thereby attempt to manage the pace of its internal adjustment to changed international circumstances. As long as states remained responsible for national security as they themselves defined it, the legality of such options—their essential legitimacy—remained crucial.

In short, freer capital movements across borders were to be encouraged in the context of a liberal international economy, but states retained the right to impede that movement whenever they themselves determined that conditions so warranted. In the decade after the formation of the OECD, the importance states attached to that right became evident.

In the wake of persistent current account imbalances experienced throughout the late 1960s and early 1970s, most industrial states in fact placed controls on short-term capital movements. Even the United States, the chief proponent of freer international capital flows throughout the postwar period, embarked on a series of experiments designed to control disequilibrating outflows and defend the pegged exchange rate system designed at Bretton Woods.[34] Increasingly, however, these flows were being channeled through markets over which it could not exert unilateral control.

Not truly divorced from more tightly regulated national financial markets, the so-called euromarkets reflected the willingness of national authorities to provide tax and other incentives for the booking of "offshore" financial transactions. The United States and its principal economic partners proved unwilling to bear the costs of shutting those markets down or of reining in the multinational corporate operations through which a rising amount of capital now effectively flowed. Unsurprisingly, therefore, more limited measures did not succeed in saving the Bretton Woods arrangements for exchange rates.

In truth, behind seemingly unstoppable speculative international capital flows lay an enduring disagreement between leading states over the distribution of adjustment burdens under conditions of tightening economic interdependence.[35] The disagreement played itself out at the level of ideas—the United States pushing for free market principles and long-run capital decontrol, the Continental Europeans and the Japanese more readily disposed toward market intervention and a higher degree of regulation. Underneath the debate lay questions of power, both within particular states and among them. Constrained now by Wall Street's overwhelming opposition to capital controls, American negotiators would have found it difficult to accept the European and Japanese position even if they had agreed with it in principle, which they did not.[36] It is important to note, however, that as the system was collapsing, multilateral discussions continued on the issue of regulating capital flows.

The discussions took place in 1972 in an ad hoc intergovernmental forum on international monetary reform. In what was labeled the "Committee of Twenty," drawn from the major constituencies of the Board of Governors of the IMF, a staff taken from the finance ministries and central banks of the leading monetary powers did the real work; they in turn assigned a group of technical experts to examine the problem of speculative capital flows. Despite difficulties encountered in specifying the extent of the problem, the final report of that group in 1974 conceded that disequilibrating flows could continue to disrupt even flexible exchange-rate arrangements. It concluded, however, that although capital controls could not be forsworn, they should not become permanent features of any new system because of their potentially damaging effect on trade and beneficial investment flows. In this connection, the group also recommended that governments seek to draft a new code of conduct for the use of capital controls and that the code be monitored by an international agency such as the IMF. This recommendation was not followed up.

To the frustration of reformers, the final report of the Committee of Twenty did not lay the groundwork for a new monetary system.[37] In the end, all that proved politically feasible was an amendment to the Articles of Agreement of the IMF which legalized floating exchange rates and gave up on trying to achieve a new consensus on the definition and management of disequilibrating capital flows. Even that outcome, however, proved to be contingent upon a rearticulation of the key normative compromise hammered out at Bretton Woods—that states were accountable to one another for the external consequences of their economic policies. The main transmission belts for those consequences were now burgeoning international capital markets. Those markets nevertheless still rested on a political foundation, for no one had elected the bankers.

The Reinvention of Multilateral Economic Surveillance

*I*F VOLUNTARY CONSULTATIONS UNDER ARTICLE VIII OF THE IMF'S charter and the obligatory analog under Article XIV established new machinery for international monetary collaboration, they did not prove capable of preventing the demolition of the central pillar of the Bretton Woods order in the early 1970s. The story of the breakdown of the "par value" exchange-rate system and the failure of subsequent attempts to craft a replacement on the basis of a new and comprehensive global bargain, a new Bretton Woods, has spawned a substantial body of research. Insofar as the expansion of international capital flows unanticipated at Bretton Woods lit the fuse for that demolition, Chapter 2 introduced key themes of that work. This chapter explores the institutional consequence at the international level of the frustrating yet continuing effort to reform the system in a coherent and comprehensive manner.

Note at the outset a crucial matter of labeling. By the lights of the original idealism of Bretton Woods and by the standards of true believers in the Fund, the word that has conventionally been used to describe the reform effort of the 1970s and beyond is "failure." The crisis for the exchange-rate system as a whole came early in the decade, and in a protracted series of negotiations Fund staff were relegated to secondary roles. But negotiations did not lead to an abandonment of the Fund. To the contrary, they led to a profound transformation inside the organization and to an expansion, potentially vast, in the scope of its core mandate. By the standards of the League of Nations under not entirely dissimilar conditions of systemic flux, the monetary reform exercise of the 1970s was a clear success. It remains true, however, that the member-states of the Fund did not match the expansion of the Fund's formal mandate with an expansion of its substantive political authority. Nor did they refrain from experimenting with new mechanisms for policy collaboration and coordination outside the Fund. Why?

The ascendancy of the capital mobility objective on the part of leading states, the standard answer in economics textbooks, provides only part of the answer. The trick is for states to move toward that objective without ceding ultimate political authority. Global financial markets can be approached only to the extent they can be rendered politically legitimate. The member-states of the League, working through the League, could not accomplish this. The member-states of the IMF learned from the earlier experience. An intergovernmental organization with nearly universal membership, committed staff, and an expansive agenda could be useful. It could be more effective than the League. But it could never be autonomous.

States marched collectively toward the breakdown of the Bretton Woods system, but the United States took the final steps alone. Between 1971, when it ceased converting the dollar into gold at fixed prices, and 1973, when it finally gave up attempts to repeg its exchange rates, the United States refused to subordinate its domestic priorities to the requirements for international monetary stability. That refusal is conventionally assigned the blame for destroying the financial rules of the early post–World War II era. Although scholarly debate continues, observers at the time made a great deal of the contempt regarding monetary obligations demonstrated on August 15, 1971 by President Richard Nixon and his treasury secretary, John Connally. In retrospect, however, it is now patently obvious that the patched-up exchange rate mechanism of the time had long since been fatally compromised by the contradiction inherent in the provision of international liquidity by way of a confidence-shattering U.S. payments deficit.

U.S. authorities nevertheless did seem to underestimate the ultimate costs of their decisions to let the value of the dollar adjust itself to the ebb and flow of international capital movements.[1] This miscalculation helps explain their subsequent obsession with reestablishing the political foundations for monetary obligations. The Fund was reborn in this context.

The Rebirth of the Fund

The record of international monetary diplomacy after 1973 suggests the rapid emergence, especially in the United States but also inside other leading states, of a desire to restore the rule of law to the post–Bretton Woods world. Hypocrisy may well be the homage vice pays to virtue, but it couldn't be helped. Without a shared sense of legitimacy in the monetary arena, the same policymakers who abrogated the central obligations of the original Bretton Woods agreement soon concluded, international trade and investment could begin a downward spiral. At a time when special import surcharges, temporary tariffs, and accusations of currency manipulation provided grist for daily headline mills, such a risk did not seem abstract. International monetary disarray appeared quite capable of restoring the world of the 1930s.

The conclusion of the League's depression studies was resurrected. In the absence of coordination in the basic national economic policies that influenced exchange rates, in the absence of a modicum of shared understandings to guide that coordination, and in the presence of freer international capital flows, movement toward deepening interdependence could be reversed.[2] Reenter the International Monetary Fund, and its ready-made apparatus for consultations.

Although the Fund itself had been ignored at critical points in the early 1970s, its Executive Board began to reemerge as a potentially important forum in 1974. After extended debate that year, it found consensus on "Guidelines for the Management of Floating Exchange Rates."[3] That the guidelines would be weak surprised no one privy to the debate, in which executive directors from countries letting their exchange rates float indicated a reluctance to grant the Fund any binding authority over their exchange-rate policies. Many even refused to go along with prior consultation, that is, with the idea that the Fund had to be consulted before a national decision was taken to move, for example, from a fluctuating to a pegged exchange rate. Still, the renewed drive to bring discussion of exchange rates and their management back to the Fund was significant.

Despite their weakness, the guidelines did establish precedents central to the recovery and expansion of the Fund's surveillance role. After specifying that members should act to "prevent or moderate" sharp, disruptive fluctuations in their exchange rates through intervention in exchange markets, they attempted to discourage policies having the intent of manipulating rates over a longer term. The guidelines also made it clear in principle that the appropriate purview of the Fund extended beyond narrow intervention practices to broader policies that had the same effect when adopted for balance-of-payments purposes, such as capital restrictions, various types of fiscal intervention, and interest-rate policies.[4] More fundamentally, the existence of the guidelines served as a reminder that only the forum of the Fund provided the near-universal membership necessary for the reestablishment of legality in the arena of exchange rates.

The guidelines themselves were clearly no substitute for a broken multilateral treaty. Only a binding new treaty could provide the sense of legitimacy that had been lost. As policymakers struggled to craft such an agreement, they had to deal with interrelated complexities. Some aspired to a new Bretton Woods, a holistic effort to treat simultaneously and under new circumstances the liquidity, adjustment, and confidence problems that all successful monetary systems must address. As it turned out, the agenda proved too ambitious and the global reform effort foundered. In substantial part this turn of events had to do with the absence of an understanding among the leading monetary powers on the utility of freer international capital movements. Without such an understanding, and given the strong preference all simultaneously evinced for autonomy in the setting of their basic economic policies, there was no chance—theoretical or political—of reaching a comprehensive agreement on exchange-rate stability. Still, among the leading monetary powers, the momentum engendered by exploratory talks was sufficient to propel a second-best solution.

In August 1975, the United States took the lead in pushing for the restoration of international monetary legality on whatever minimal basis could now be achieved. The United States, the United Kingdom, France, the Federal Republic of Germany, and Japan first attempted to reach agreement among themselves on key issues, the most contentious of which was the nature of the exchange-rate regime. Since France and the United States had previously articulated the most divergent positions on that issue, after a series of frustrating discussions their exasperated colleagues agreed to go along with any agreement they might hammer out between them.[5]

Although their positions had been moderating over time, France was the key proponent of a return to some version of a fixed rate system, whereas the United States insisted on retaining its ability to let the dollar float. Not coincidentally, France was inclined to support capital controls, whereas the United States most vociferously was not. Differing positions on a range of technical monetary issues complicated the subsequent negotiations, but significant doctrinal differences regarding the relationship between state institutions and the market were obviously at work also. The search for middle ground between the two positions essentially came down to a series of secret meetings in the fall of 1975 between the undersecretary of the U.S. Treasury, Edwin Yeo, and the deputy finance minister of France and future managing director of the IMF, Jacques de Larosière.[6]

On the surface, the negotiations between Yeo and de Larosière seemed a search for a technical bridge between the American and French positions. The bridge would take the form of a formal amendment to the IMF's Articles of Agreement. Under the surface, however, they were about what international monetary disputes are always about—*how* the burden of adjustment should be distributed among countries with external payments deficits and countries with external payments surpluses. The two sides needed words that would accommodate their very different worldviews and very different ideas on how to manage the domestic adjustments necessitated by external economic involvement. On the surface, the negotiations were about designing an arcane text, the flexible interpretation of which could attract broad support. Underneath the surface, they constituted an important and readily understandable effort to determine whether post-1973 international monetary arrangements would constitute a legitimate order. Much more than technical niceties was involved. The abrogation of the previous rules in the early 1970s had opened a Pandora's box. The specter of monetary anarchy of the type that helped destroy the original aspirations of the League of Nations came out of that box. Negotiations now were about coaxing the specter back in, closing the lid, and enhancing the probability that the box would not be reopened any time soon.

The political battle lines were easy to see. Consistent with traditional French views, de Larosière believed that the Americans enjoyed an "exorbitant privilege" in their ability as a reserve center to finance their external deficits with their own currency. As Charles de Gaulle never tired of arguing, they had abused that privilege, an abuse evident in widening internal and external imbalances and in rising inflation. A banker by profession, Yeo had some sympathy for the view that external discipline would not necessarily be a bad thing for the United States. His bargaining position, however, was informed by keen political instinct. For Yeo, it was not only appropriate but essential that other countries, especially those with persistent payments surpluses like Germany and Japan, bear more of the costs of international adjustment.

Within the U.S. Congress, such a view had been advanced for many years, and quite energetically, by Henry Reuss, the respected and influential chairman of the House Banking Committee. On international monetary matters, his colleagues deferred to him, and his firm view was that any constraints on the ability of the United States to redistribute those costs should be resisted. Reuss also frequently noted, however, that such resistance had to confront the possibility that the fallback tool for that redistribution—floating exchange rates—could destabilize the world trading system by making it easier for countries to manipulate their currencies.

With an eye on the Congress, which would have to ratify his handiwork, Yeo found a way around the conundrum. He advocated not stable exchange rates, which the French preferred, but a "stable system of exchange rates." How would such a "stable system" be maintained in the absence of a binding rule? The American answer was twofold: leave it up to individual countries to create the conditions for domestic price stability, and renew and expand the mandate of the IMF to exercise "surveillance" over the adjustment process.[7] The key Bretton Woods assumption had been that the necessity of defending a pegged exchange rate overseen by the Fund would encourage internal policy adjustments to external economic developments. This new rationale effectively assumed, on the contrary, that international market forces supplemented by peer pressure embodied in the Fund would discipline countries and foster domestic conditions conducive to international stability.

In the end, in the face of U.S. intransigence and accepting the unfeasibility of repegging exchange rates at a time when wide differences existed in national levels of inflation, France was prepared to accept this thinking. De Larosière insisted, however, that the word "firm" precede "surveillance" in the final text. He also insisted that the text not preclude the possibility of the eventual restoration of pegged rates.[8]

The word "surveillance" was chosen with care. Proposed as early as 1973 in the context of the abortive exercise in multilateral reform then under way, it had been tested under fire. Two years before the Yeo–de Larosière negotiations, Congressman Reuss had become extremely exercised about the word in public hearings. He objected strongly to the possibility that the ability of the United States to let its exchange rate float might at some point be constrained by an IMF empowered to "exercise surveillance." Paul Volcker, then undersecretary of the treasury, riposted, "Now I do not object to 'surveillance.' I think a country operating on a floating rate should be subjected to some international rules and surveillance."[9] Other terms, among them "management" and "regulation," were considered, but all were rejected since they implied deference by nation-states to a higher authority. To Arthur Burns, the powerful chairman of the U.S. Federal Reserve, surveillance had the right "connotation," a conclusion Reuss eventually came to accept. No one ever successfully explained to Reuss or to anyone else, however, the difference between "surveillance" and "firm surveillance."[10]

In November 1975, the text of the agreement between France and the United States, after some refinement by Joseph Gold and other key officials at the Fund, was blessed at the Rambouillet summit of the leading monetary powers. Attending were the heads of government of the so-called Group of Five plus Italy, a precursor to what would become the Group of Seven when Canada was added. In January 1976, it received formal assent from the IMF's inaptly named Interim Committee, the new policymaking body interposed between its titular Board of Governors, which included the finance ministers or central bank governors of all of its members, and its Executive Board, which managed day-to-day operations. The text became the key item—Article IV—in the Second Amendment to the Articles of Agreement of the Fund, which upon ratification would restore the monetary system to legality.

The text of new Article IV enjoined the Fund to "oversee the international monetary system in order to ensure its effective operation" as well as to "exercise firm surveillance over the exchange rate policies of members, and . . . adopt specific principles for the guidance of all members with respect to those policies." Moreover, those principles were to "respect the domestic social and political policies of members, and when applying these principles, the Fund shall pay due regard to the circumstances of members." Those members were, for their part, required to "provide the Fund with the information necessary for such surveillance, and, when requested by the Fund, [to] consult with it on . . . exchange rate policies." In formal terms, Article VIII and Article XIV countries were put on an equal footing; whether their currencies were fully convertible or not, all were now obliged to participate in Fund consultations. Finally, the text enjoined all members to "avoid manipulating exchange rates or the international monetary system in order to prevent effective balance of payments adjustment or to gain an unfair competitive advantage over other members."[11]

During the ratification debate that followed in the United States, Undersecretary Yeo provided insight into the reasons behind the agreement when he defended it before the Foreign Relations Committee of the Senate. He began his testimony by emphasizing the need "to restore the legal framework that is necessary . . . to reduce the risk that nations will pursue selfish policies which pay too little regard to the effects on others." In the face of skeptical questioning, he amplified this theme.

> We feel [the legislation] is important because interdependence . . . has to be governed by a body, a structure of law. I think we can all . . . feel fortunate that coming out of recession we have not in any significant degree seen or observed restrictionist tendencies or beggar-thy-neighbor tendencies. This legislation will provide a framework to insure that that performance continues. . . . The best example of what happens when countries as a group follow beggar-thy-neighbor policies was uncovered in the 1930s. Each individual country pursued its narrow interests in the most circumscribed manner imaginable—tariff barriers, competitive devaluations—and we all lost. . . . I hesitate to use the word urgent—but [it is] quite important that we go back to the rule of law in terms of the international monetary system.[12]

Note that this testimony was provided by a spokesman for a Republican and strongly market-oriented administration. Treasury Secretary William Simon, Yeo's boss, was well known for his passionate advocacy of free enterprise and competitive markets. Nevertheless, even he had come to accept the view that market discipline alone was inadequate to the task of stabilizing international monetary relations in the contemporary environment.[13] A new legal structure, however soft its actual rules, was considered worth the expenditure of so much time, negotiating effort, and political capital. In order to secure congressional assent for that structure, including its central provision for multilateral surveillance, it obviously seemed useful to raise the threat of a 1930s-style manipulation of exchange rates. There is little doubt, moreover, that key policymakers sincerely believed that the analogy was appropriate. Yeo and Sam Cross, U.S. executive director at the Fund during the Second Amendment negotiations, subsequently continued to emphasize the importance of measures to prevent states from gaining unfair competitive advantage through exchange rate manipulation.[14] At the same time, it was considered important to build significant flexibility into the structure, flexibility capable of accommodating the fact that states wanted to retain their sovereign right to opt in or out of international exchange arrangements.

The commitment to IMF surveillance by the leading monetary power thus rested on a choice between potential economic losses if competitive impulses reasserted themselves in the arena of exchange rates and an immediate and potentially expanding infringement on its domestic political authority. National economic policies that had a systemic impact would not be "constrained" by any supranational authority, but many who might initially have concurred with Henry Reuss on the sanctity of national authority had eventually come to agree on the necessity of a limitation expressed in terms of external accountability. A supportive political coalition rested on a sense of disquiet concerning the viability of the status quo, a world without a modicum of agreed monetary order. The 1930s analogy, despite its debatable appropriateness in far different economic circumstances, gave that sense a clearer meaning.

On paper, and broadly interpreted, the new Articles of Agreement seemed to give the Fund a significantly expanded role.[15] In practice, the resistance of member-states to the granting of effective new powers to the Fund was intense. In the post-ratification discussions of the Fund's Executive Board on the design of a substantive code of conduct that would make the new Article IV operative and replace the loose 1974 guidelines on floating, deep divisions immediately appeared.

In a series of background papers, the managing director and staff of the Fund subtly pushed for a broad interpretation to revive the notion of prior consultation before changes in exchange rates that were not floating, to permit the Fund to take a view on whether an exchange rate was "wrong" or creating "disorderly" market conditions, and to facilitate Fund inquiries into a wider range of domestic policies.[16] A second approach, identified with Continental European members, rejected prior consultation but called for the Fund to promote broad policy objectives by, for example, taking a view on the correctness of particular exchange rates.[17] Countering both of these views, the United States, Canada, and Britain favored an approach that would defer to market forces, narrowly construe the meaning of market disorder, and concentrate the Fund's mandate on the prevention of exchange-rate manipulation by governments.[18] In the face of these differences, it was obvious that a set of clear or encompassing principles would be impossible to design. On the basis of a suggestion from the Canadians and the British, indeed, all that could be agreed at this initial stage was that a 1974-style "guidelines" approach might allow specific principles to evolve out of practice. Following extended study and debate along these lines, and cognizant of fundamental consensus only on the illegitimacy of currency manipulation and of a general distaste for Fund meddling in the internal affairs of members, the "First Surveillance Decision" finally emerged from the board in April 1977.[19]

Echoing themes expressed at Bretton Woods, the 1977 decision really articulated only one formally binding principle—that members *shall* not manipulate exchange rates or the system as a whole in order to avoid adjustment or to gain a competitive advantage. Two nonbinding principles complemented it: that members *should* intervene in exchange markets to counter disorderly conditions, and that members *should* take into account in their intervention policies the interests of other members. Beyond this interpretation of the new Article IV commitments, the significance of the 1977 decision lay in its explication of a practical mechanism for monitoring adherence. Members agreed in the decision to consult with the Fund annually on their exchange-rate policies. In effect, these consultations subsumed those previously held under Article VIII or XIV. Hereafter, none was voluntary.

In view of the key objective of encouraging adjustment of imbalances in international payments, the 1977 decision specified a series of developments that would suggest the need for additional consultations with the Fund, including protracted large-scale intervention, unsustainable levels of borrowing, the introduction or substantial modification of restrictions on capital flows, the use of monetary and other domestic financial policies that gave abnormal encouragement to capital flows, and so on. To appraise such developments, the Fund was formally empowered to inquire into a range of policies that had an impact on exchange rates.

The 1977 decision called on the Fund, in exercising its new powers, to recognize that members' objectives included not just international adjustment but also "sustained sound economic growth and reasonable levels of employment."[20] Additionally, in a weak replacement for the former requirement that a member consult with the Fund before changing its exchange rate, the decision gave the managing director the authority to question, at his own initiative, the exchange-rate policies of members and report to the executive directors on the answers.[21] In later years, this authority would justify the involvement of the managing director in restricted discussions on economic policy coordination held outside the Fund. Finally, the decision authorized periodic global reviews of exchange-rate and related economic developments, a task that now culminates in the annual publication of the Fund's *World Economic Outlook* and other surveys. Harking back to the League's *World Economic Survey,* those publications provide the most visible aspect of the Fund's surveillance role.

The Second Amendment to the Fund's Articles and the Surveillance Decision of 1977 replaced the Bretton Woods regime with what has been called "soft law."[22] Fund members now agreed that the modicum of policy coordination conducive to international economic prosperity could best be promoted not by specific rules but by procedural adaptation. In subtle ways, such an approach extended the legal jurisdiction of the Fund by expanding the scope of its consultations process. Moreover, all consultations were now to end with a summing-up by the managing director, which after any amendments by directors was to become a formal legal statement of the board. More significant, despite the apparent narrowness of the 1977 decision, the explicit recognition that broader, macroeconomic policies had an important impact on exchange rates in the increasingly liberal policy environment of the 1980s and 1990s would actually widen considerably the purview of the Fund.

This turned out to be a key development. As national financial policies moved in the general direction of liberalization, the consequences for exchange rates gave the Fund a keen interest in the international capital markets thereby promoted. That interest gave the Fund, even though its explicit mandate remained confined to the current account of national payments balances, a natural and logical role to play in overseeing developments in capital accounts. As we shall see, such a role subsequently came to the fore as the Fund helped manage the developing country debt crisis of the 1980s and its analog in the 1990s.

In a major review of the 1977 decision undertaken in 1995, the Executive Board took several steps to improve the flow of data into the Fund and to streamline its analysis of financial market developments. Significantly, it also amended the original decision to enable the Fund to inquire into the causes of "unsustainable flows of private capital." Although this amendment stopped short of granting formal powers over national capital accounts to the Fund, it did acknowledge an expansion in the scope of the Fund's surveillance function in practice, a development made possible by the 1977 decision.[23]

That the formal surveillance mandate of the Fund would meet resistance has always been certain. External advice on politically sensitive economic policies is not always welcome. Ameliorating resistance in the post–Bretton Woods era, however, was broad acceptance by the Fund's membership of a certain point of view. At a time when market signals, especially financial market signals, were increasingly allowed to guide national economic policymaking—and, moreover, in a world lacking consensus on exchange-rate arrangements—multilateral economic surveillance was more, not less, necessary. The fundamental incentive to accept such a view later became crystal clear.

In a world of states, markets channel national power. They buffer political choices by diffusing and depersonalizing responsibility for their consequences. Just as independent central banks buffer governments while remaining part of the state, so markets buffer the state without necessarily usurping ultimate political authority. The day-to-day workings of markets may obscure the fact that political choices have been made, but they do not substitute for them. The experience of the League suggested that stable markets required the collabora-tive deployment of the political authority of states. It also suggested that a crucial part of that deployment involved systemic oversight and crisis management. The buffer of the market itself required a buffer.

Surveillance and the Fund's Other Roles

The surveillance function of the Fund is today intimately related to its more public functions, which include the provision of tempo-rary balance-of-payments financing and technical advisory services to members in need. Article IV consultations and associated eco-nomic analyses establish a basis for the "stand-by" arrangements the Fund negotiates with members that have problems matching the pro-ceeds of their exports and incoming investments with the costs of their imports and outgoing investments.[24] Those consultations also provide a framework for a broad range of advice to members that request it, for example, on central banking procedures, the prepa-ration of national statistical accounts, and so on. That framework, in turn, is shaped by broader Fund analyses, including the *World Eco-nomic Outlook* and various other staff studies.

As the postwar system evolved, exchange-rate stability—the Fund's original raison d'être—obviously proved an elusive goal. It may even have been an unwise goal, given the role that exchange-rate adjust-ments, effectively coordinated across states, can play in helping to ad-dress national payments imbalances. One difficulty was to encourage such adjustments at times when the credibility of a government was at stake. When that issue could be dealt with, a more serious difficul-ty was to prevent a government from manipulating exchange rates in pursuit of commercial advantage. Be that as it may, by the 1970s exchange-rate stability had clearly become a secondary policy objec-tive for the system leader, the United States. National policy auton-omy and international capital mobility had moved up in the pecking order. When the crisis of the early 1970s finally arrived, the Americans chose to jettison the central exchange-rate plank of the Bretton Woods architecture, leaving the Fund, as we saw, in a legal twilight zone.

While its constitutional base was under revision, the Fund nevertheless continued with various operations designed to promote liberal financial policies conducive both to full currency convertibility and to openness in national payment systems conducive to expanding world trade and investment. The consultations process that became the center of the Fund's renewed surveillance function in the mid-1970s served this goal in substantial part. So too did technical advisory missions aimed at establishing efficient systems of economic and monetary management within member-states. Working in the same direction were the Fund's own financing programs, which over time became ever more ambitious.

The Fund has never been the main provider of the financial grease that keeps the machinery of international commerce working smoothly. In the early postwar period, the purchasing power of a burgeoning American economy helped fill this need, as did the Marshall Plan and other intergovernmental transfers. Soon, international capital markets also reemerged. Nevertheless, the Fund has long supplemented international liquidity with resources provided by its members.

In the beginning, those resources were limited to quota subscriptions pledged to the Fund, not unlike the equity subscribed to a private bank by its shareholders. In 1961, the ten leading member-states, through their central banks, supplemented this funding by providing the Fund with the capacity to borrow from themselves to agreed levels. Switzerland, a nonmember of the Fund, supplemented these "general arrangements to borrow" in 1964. The contributors became known as the Group of Ten. Outside these arrangements, Saudi Arabia and other oil-exporting states expanded the Fund's pool of borrowed resources in the mid-1970s, as did Japan in later years.

The politics behind the financing of the Fund itself are as complicated as they are obscure. But three points deserve emphasis before we highlight the connection between the organization's overall financial role and its changing surveillance function. First, quotas establish an internal pecking order among Fund members. Voting power in the Fund is determined by these quotas, and their distribution is weighted. The aim is to avoid the gridlock and inertia that historically plagued organizations like the League, which required unanimity for important decisions, while accommodating the fact that power is distributed unevenly among states. Although most issues inside the Fund are decided through consensual procedures, everyone knows the way votes would come out if they had to be taken. For particularly significant decisions, such as a change in the Fund's Articles, an 85 percent majority is required. Any member or group of members capable of mustering 15 percent therefore enjoys the ability to block such decisions. In the mid-1990s, the United States accounted for 18 percent of Fund quotas; collectively the leading industrial states comprising the Group of Seven accounted for 47 percent.

The second point worth underlining concerns the degree of leverage inherent in the two mechanisms for expanding the Fund's financial resources. Once increased quotas are approved, the Fund can use the proceeds at its discretion, subject to the rules specified in its Articles and in the decisions of its board. In theory, the membership retains the ability to withdraw its quota subscriptions, but in practice this is unlikely. Borrowed resources, however, may more readily be controlled by the members putting them at the Fund's disposal. They are also easier to arrange. Quota increases, although strongly preferred by the Fund, sometimes entail legislative affirmation within member-states. They certainly do in the United States, a reality which has complicated the life of the Fund since the beginning. Credit lines, however, may be put into place directly by central banks or by finance ministries under executive order. Akin to deposits and other liabilities on the balance sheet of a private bank, borrowed resources enable the Fund to meet its requirements while subtly shifting the locus of control within the organization even further away from debtor states and Fund officials and toward creditor states. Since 1961, this shift has been symbolized in the economic policy consultations that members of the Group of Ten and the even more exclusive Group of Seven regularly hold among themselves outside the auspices of the Fund.

The final point to note is that by whatever measure, Fund quotas and borrowing arrangements as a proportion of international reserves available to industrialized and most industrializing states have become much smaller in comparison to the financing available through burgeoning international capital markets. In other words, as discussed in Chapter 2, during the past few decades states that are net lenders have chosen to provide reserves to net borrowers mainly through private capital markets. To the extent they have chosen to supplement the international reserves available to debtors, lenders have done so in part through expanding the Fund's borrowing capability. As we shall see, borrowers in turn often shy away from the Fund because its assistance comes with conditions attached. For exactly that reason, however, lenders have sometimes been willing to channel resources through it. And partly to exert as much influence as possible over those conditions themselves, they often prefer to provide the Fund with debt instead of equity.

Although the seeds of the Fund's financing operations were sown in the original Articles of Agreement, the precise manner in which they sprouted was not anticipated in 1944. If they could be reassembled now, few of the delegates at Bretton Woods would be surprised by the evolution of the Fund's technical advisory role. On the other hand, some would probably wonder that the Fund's surveillance function now involves it in halting efforts among the leading industrial states to coordinate the full range of their macroeconomic policies. Most, however, would likely be stunned by the changing character of its financial role.

Since the late 1970s, only developing or formerly socialist countries have negotiated financing arrangements with the Fund. In number and duration, those arrangements have expanded dramatically. Originally meant to provide short-term assistance while members extricated themselves from liquidity problems, Fund assistance now comes in many varieties, including medium-term loans to assist members grappling with deeper structural difficulties. In general, stand-by arrangements from the Fund, which specify certain policy commitments designed to promote adjustment, have come to be seen by private financiers as providing a "seal of approval." That seal can open the door to future financing through private markets.

As the Fund's role as a financial intermediary for certain members expanded over time, the conditions attached to its financing became the subject of much controversy. The practical origins of Fund "conditionality" can be traced to a proposal made in 1952 by Ivar Rooth, the Fund's second managing director. Looking to spur the Fund out of the doldrums of its early years, when the United States chose not to use the institution in the major tasks of financial reconstruction, the Rooth plan enabled the Fund's resources to be used under arrangements negotiated with individual members on a case-by-case basis. Small amounts could be drawn at minimal cost, whereas larger drawings would incur higher charges and explicit expectations regarding appropriate changes in national policies.

The plan succeeded in reviving interest in the Fund and established a precedent for all financing programs designed by the Fund in later years. It also provided the United States with a new lever for encouraging currency convertibility. Conditions to that effect were attached to drawings from the Fund, conditions that proved more palatable when they came from an organization in which the borrowers had a degree of influence than when they came by fiat from the United States.

Although it was not labeled as "surveillance" in the Fund's early days, this ability to match the carrot of financial resources with the stick of conditionality gave Fund oversight its first concrete shape. But the Fund's resources were limited and, as noted, compared to the size of international capital markets they became smaller over time. The question soon arose, therefore, as to how those resources could best be allocated. On this point, Susan Strange first captured the essence of the answer over twenty years ago.

> By a series of small, local, operational decisions, which appeared to those involved to be of a routine, precedent-following kind, a policy was slowly hammered out, which applied the Fund's resources in a highly political manner. Without its ever being stated in so many words, the Fund's operational decisions made its resources available neither to those in the greatest need nor to those with the best record of good behavior in keeping to

the rules, but paradoxically to those members whose financial difficulties were most likely to jeopardize the stability of
the international monetary system.[25]

With its financing role shaped in this fashion, the Fund's capacity to provide surveillance developed, quite by accident, into an incipient capacity to manage systemic crises in a world of expanding
international capital markets.

Surveillance, Financing, and Crisis Management

In a sense, of course, the Fund has always been involved in financial
crises; under a regime of pegged exchange rates, every major exchange-
rate realignment constituted a crisis of sorts for the particular governments involved. But only in the past fifteen years has the Fund's
role as crisis manager fully developed. In the midst of the developing
country debt crisis that began in 1982 and the transitions to capitalism in the former Soviet Union and its allies later in the decade, that
role came to constitute a primary rationale for the continued existence of the Fund. In an era when international capital markets might
have been expected to render superfluous its financing role, the Fund
and its surveillance mandate became more, not less, important. Like
adaptations within the League during the 1920s, this did not happen
by design.

Crisis management implies the need for speed and suppleness,
but the Fund is a bureaucratic institution guided by precedent and
encumbered by a tradition of consensus decision making. In the contemporary period, however, one innovation made it possible for the
Fund to close the gap between systemic needs and organizational
capabilities. Partly by force of personality and partly by the willing
acquiescence of leading member-states, the managing director became increasingly prominent in the Fund's policymaking machinery. The underlying rationale for this new development derived from
the Fund's surveillance mandate as it had reemerged in the late 1970s.
Upon this foundation, the managing director and the increasingly

sophisticated analytical team behind him became key proponents of a new intellectual consensus on national economic policies appropriate in an era of heightened international capital mobility. The "Washington consensus," the terms of which will be discussed later, was not actually as fresh as it seemed, for its roots extended back to a time the managing director's political overseers had long forgotten. A brief look at the Fund's role in recent international financial emergencies indicates important lines of adaptation in the process of multilateral economic surveillance.

The word "management" is often used to describe the role of the Fund in the debt crisis of the 1980s. It is appropriate. Relieved celebrations in the international financial community marked the tenth anniversary of Mexico's 1982 repayment moratorium. For most of the people actually caught up in it, however, the ensuing crisis was during that decade managed, not finally resolved. As Mexico itself found out late in 1994, when a massive new outflow of capital forced it to devalue its currency and adopt harsh austerity measures, underlying problems survived. But of course it was not really the end of the crisis that private financiers celebrated in 1992 and once again during the fiftieth-anniversary commemorations of the Bretton Woods Conference a couple of years later. Most were remembering the near-collapse of the international payment system and its avoidance. Others, no doubt, were recalling their own extrication from the business of development financing.

The managing director of the Fund at the time the crisis broke was Jacques de Larosière, the erstwhile French negotiator of the new Article IV a few years before. In brokering a deal that effectively rescheduled Mexico's excessive debt to foreign banks and provided a precedent for other heavily indebted countries, he demonstrated the utility of having a credible multilateral organization in place to confront future emergencies in increasingly integrated financial markets. Contrary to common perceptions, at base the Fund did not play a lender-of-last-resort function, and de Larosière was not the world's central banker. Although his organization's credibility was enhanced by the fact that it had its own financial resources to contribute to the final deal, its true function was to buffer the real lenders of last resort, the governments and central banks of the leading industrial states. The job of the managing director, handled with aplomb by de Larosière, was to help stabilize the international capital markets that now mediated the relationships between creditor states and debtor states. Failure would not only have disrupted the markets, it would also have profoundly challenged the legitimacy of prior decisions by those states to rely on those markets.

When Mexico's finance minister, Jesus Silva Herzog, came to Washington on August 13, 1982, to discuss the imminent prospect of his country's defaulting on its external debts, he called on the U.S. Federal Reserve, the Treasury, and de Larosière.[26] Over the course of drawn-out and complex negotiations, a Fund stand-by arrangement became the pivot around which a comprehensive debt restructuring package for Mexico was assembled. De Larosière's function was described by Paul Volcker, then chairman of the U.S. Federal Reserve, as that of a "bankruptcy judge on a grand international scale."[27] This was an overstatement, of course, since de Larosière had no power to compel creditors to grant concessions. Still, the Fund could provide some cash to Mexico to forestall default, and it could attach conditions to that cash. This is what it promised to do if the country's foreign bank creditors themselves put up more loans and deferred their expectations of repayment.

In short, the banks' individual instincts told them to declare Mexico in default and attempt to seize whatever assets they could, but de Larosière helped persuade them to give the country time potentially to grow out of its debt problem. At the same time, he assured them that Fund surveillance would encourage policy movement in Mexico conducive to achieving that goal. As Volcker put it:

> De Larosière did something that had not been done before, and something that set the basic financing framework for dealing with the debt crisis. He insisted that no Fund program or loan for Mexico would be approved without the commercial banks first committing to a "critical mass" of the needed bank financing, which was set at 90% of the total loans that commercial banks were expected to produce.... The effect was to force a high degree of solidarity among the lending banks.[28]

True to his calling, Volcker is being diplomatic. One official present at a meeting on November 16, 1982, where de Larosière explained to the bankers that they would be expected to put up $5 billion of the total $8.3 billion refinancing package, recalled the moment more graphically: "It caused a kind of frenzy."[29] The frenzy subsided considerably when Volcker himself gave the approach his official sanction and made it known that new loans to Mexico would be treated leniently for regulatory purposes.[30] The reason was easy to fathom. Defaults on old and new loans would wipe out more than the entire capital bases of the biggest American banks. Ultimately, de Larosière's threat to walk away from the deal had the desired effect. Mexico now had a slim chance to kick-start the engines of economic growth, and the banks now had the time to build up their loan-loss provisions.

The projection of the Fund into the center of the debt crisis ultimately depended, of course, on much more than the forceful personality of the managing director. It reflected the strategy of the U.S. government to avoid, redistribute, or at the very least postpone the financial and political burdens it would face if Mexico and other Latin American debtors defaulted. Together with other leading states whose cooperation was important to the success of the effort, it also had a more fundamental reason. Having collectively built an international economic system around more deeply connected national financial markets, leading states had a common interest in avoiding the disintegration of those markets.

Focusing minds most acutely in the United States was the prospect of a collapse of the domestic banking system.[31] Congress, ever uppermost in the minds of Federal Reserve and Treasury policymakers, had found such reasoning compelling ever since 1929. The influence of that specter was particularly evident now, when the power and resources of the U.S. government itself were perceived by many to be much more constrained than they had been. Thus the real game in Washington during the 1980s was about buffering the government and the economy of the United States as completely as possible and for as long as possible from the unintended implications of strategic decisions taken long ago to promote the integration of American and foreign financial markets.

Based on close interviews with participants, one journalist's account nicely summarizes the politics of the situation.

> From the beginning, says Deputy Treasury Secretary Tim McNamar, the Treasury made a decision never to "ask the banks to put another nickel into these countries because the minute the Treasury does that, they're our loans." Instead the Treasury left the dirty work to the Fed because "the Fed is not part of the government." Volcker and other central bankers, in turn, were relieved to have the IMF provide a political shield for them by going out front. "De Larosière was better placed to do some things," elaborates one high Fed official. "He could demand cooperation from the financial community. As an international civil servant, his role as the 'heavy' further depoliticized the process."[32]

More important, the Fund and its surveillance apparatus could also play the role of "heavy" with indebted countries. It could not force policy changes, but it could encourage changes in a way that was less of an affront to national sensitivities than direct interventions by the authorities of another state. In this respect, the logic was exactly the same as that behind League involvement in Central Europe during the 1920s. The main differences lay in the fact that the Fund could bring its own financial resources to bear and in the broader legal foundation on which its surveillance mandate rested.

Before and after de Larosière left the Fund in 1986, the organization used its financial resources and its surveillance procedures ever more intensively in various indebted countries. On the one hand, the moral authority conferred by its multilateral surveillance mandate was deployed to marshal financial resources and regulatory flexibility in creditor countries; on the other hand, the conditionality attached to its own lending, and by extension to private credits attracted by that lending, was used to encourage policy reformulation in indebted countries.[33]

By the late 1980s, however, it had become painfully evident that the basic strategy was not working. Most heavily indebted countries did not face liquidity problems susceptible to the medicine of economic growth. With expanding burdens of debt repayment in the fifteen heavily indebted countries then at the center of the crisis, the idea that they could grow their way out of their problems was exposed as a sham. Early in 1989, therefore, the U.S. treasury secretary proposed to use the resources of the Fund and the World Bank to assist countries interested in "buying back" their bank debt. Michel Camdessus, who succeeded de Larosière as managing director of the Fund, embraced the new strategy, and once again the Fund's involvement proved crucial to its implementation.

Extinguishing debt at the international level is part of a long tradition. During the bank lending spree that followed the jacking up of world oil prices in the early 1970s, Walter Wriston, then chairman of Citibank, used to say that "countries don't go broke." But of course they do. Many have in history. And in the 1980s, many did again. The debt strategy of the early 1980s successfully shielded the economies of net creditors by giving their banks time to buy an insurance policy in the form of increased reserves. In leading states, a recapitulation of 1929 was avoided. The debt strategy of the late 1980s and early 1990s focused, with somewhat more ambiguous success, on ameliorating the consequences of default that history predicted for the debtors: the adoption of restrictive domestic policies cutting them off from external markets and a lengthy loss of access to external sources of funding. As common as they might be in history, debt reductions must themselves be paid for. The challenge of the debt crisis in its newest phase was to see whether the citizenry in indebted countries could be saved from bearing all of the costs.

In line with U.S. policy goals, Camdessus and his staff showed remarkable creativity in helping to organize the reductions of bank debt in such a way that most debtors avoided a lasting expulsion from international capital markets. The contribution of the Fund, however, turned not so much on intellectual talent as on the availability of its surveillance apparatus and the financing programs it supported. Most debtors negotiated new stand-by arrangements with the Fund, under which Fund resources and policy advice were made available subject to limits and to performance conditions specified in terms of standard macroeconomic variables. Those conditions were in line with what many now call the "Washington consensus." The advice for all countries was to adopt outward-oriented trade and investment policies, monetary policies aimed at price stability, fiscal policies aimed at balance in the medium term, unified systems of currency convertibility at realistic exchange rates, and liberal financial policies designed to build open, transparent, and solid capital markets. The incentive to move in such a direction was the promise of restructured and reduced bank debt and new financing, mainly in the form of private portfolio and direct investment. In other words, as the Fund helped usher foreign banks out, it opened the door to foreign bond purchasers, mutual funds, and multinational corporations as well as to domestic wealth-holders potentially interested in repatriating their own foreign investments.

At first glance, the Washington consensus did not differ sharply from the conclusions that League economists had reached many years before. As the second phase of the debt crisis was winding down, that point came out between the lines in a book of essays Fund staff members put together to honor Jacques Polak.[34] (Polak joined the Fund in 1947, four years after leaving the League. He rose quickly to become the head of the Fund's Research Department, from which he retired in 1979 to serve as an executive director on the Fund's board until 1986. Together with Joseph Gold in the Legal Department, Polak had played a prominent role in shaping the Fund's policy advice over many years. Both men stayed on inside the Fund as advisers to their colleagues long after their formal retirements.)

Like his colleague Ragnar Nurkse, Polak had been skeptical about assigning policy priority to the openness of capital markets, but his early work accommodated "equilibrating" capital flows between interdependent countries. Partly for this reason, the model built on his work, which has long shaped the thinking of Fund economists, accommodated the idea that exchange-rate adjustments would occasionally be essential to facilitate both internal and external balance in national accounts. Too frequent adjustments, however, threatened to undermine confidence, spark reactions in the policies of trading partners, and undercut long-run prospects for growth. Pragmatism was called for, but so too were disciplined monetary and fiscal policies. Moreover, when spillovers became common across interdependent national economies, information-sharing at least, and policy coordination at best, was necessary to stabilize the international economy and keep national markets open. The onus remained on individual countries to adjust their economies as necessary to achieve such an outcome, but multilateral intermediaries could help facilitate constructively coordinated responses from other countries.

The trouble was that the Washington consensus did not make clear what a country should do when the liberal financial policies required to deal with debt problems and attract new capital flows undermined its exchange-rate and broader macroeconomic objectives. It also did not make clear what the multilateral intermediary should do in such cases. If a pegged exchange rate had been chosen as a tool of disinflation but adjustment was later required, pressure from the intermediary might undermine confidence, prompt capital flight, and force an excessive depreciation of the exchange rate. The end result might be even higher rates of inflation. The zeal of the converted could easily overwhelm the need for pragmatic flexibility in applying the norms of the consensus, while the need for confidentiality could undermine the effectiveness of the intermediary. Market liberalization across the board could become an end in itself. Mexico, the traditional harbinger of things to come for the industrializing world, squarely confronted the resulting contradictions in 1994.

Having firmly embraced the debt restructuring and policy reforms associated with the Washington consensus in 1989, Mexico was hailed as the exemplar of successful adjustment in the early 1990s.[35] Every step of the way, it worked with the Fund. The government seemed to be doing everything right. Sound macroeconomic policies brought down inflation and created an environment conducive to solid growth. Trade and financial liberalization promised a brighter future. A nationalized banking system moved quickly toward privatization. A fixed exchange rate reassured foreign investors that their capital would not be devalued. For a time the reward was steadily rising direct investment inflows and massive inflow of portfolio capital. But in 1994, Mexico's banking system nearly collapsed, and its economy went into a tailspin.

Wishful thinking characterized much of that year. Many in Mexico, including the government, made mistakes. Creditors compounded them. Internal studies later indicated that the Fund too misread the situation. The most important symptom of looming trouble was a rapidly widening current account deficit in the mid-1990s financed by short-term capital flows. It brought the exchange rate of the peso under increasing pressure at a time when a newly liberated commercial banking system was not yet ready to deal with a confidence-shattering devaluation. In December, Mexico's central bank depleted its reserves after an attempt to manage a devaluation failed. Domestic and foreign investors ran for the recently opened door, and the peso plummeted.

The U.S. Treasury and the Federal Reserve quickly mounted a rescue operation. Their motives were not quite as straightforward as they had been in 1982, when the direct impact of Mexican-related financial losses was concentrated in the banking system. But a complex set of policy objectives, ranging from financial risk containment to fears about immigration, was obviously at work. In January 1995, the U.S. administration proposed to Congress a $40 billion package of loan guarantees to help Mexico ride out the storm. Despite support from the leadership of both the House and the Senate, a remarkable level of public disapproval led many representatives and senators to oppose the bid. The administration withdrew its request at the end of the month, and in February it cobbled together a package that did not need congressional authorization. Short-term funds at the disposal of the Treasury were used, but a crucial $18 billion came from the IMF.

The necessity for quick action prompted Camdessus to short-circuit the usual procedures for board review of new stand-by arrangements. This move caused a good deal of consternation, especially in European capitals. Even more strikingly, the rescue package implied large exceptions from normal IMF practice. The Fund's contribution turned out to be seven times larger than Mexico's normal limit, an amount that represented 20 percent of the Fund's total liquid resources. If anyone had doubts about the continuing intimacy of the relationship between the Fund and the leading state in the international economic system, these exceptions dispelled them.

The United States was driven to use the Fund by the force of political circumstances. Domestic reactions to the exigencies of increasingly integrated capital markets clearly came into conflict with broad and deep foreign policy goals significantly associated with those markets. The costs of too clear a choice were high. The IMF was available to help forestall that choice and to obfuscate it. Bending its internal rules and demonstrating that its mandate was not truly symmetrical had its own risks. As in 1982 and 1989, the Fund nevertheless retained a broadly accepted ability to attach policy strings to its financing and to follow up with tools of oversight. In the grand scheme of things, the United States preferred to risk undermining the Fund rather than risk the stability of the international capital markets now so central to its broader policies. Having long ago decided to promote those markets, the United States now confronted a challenge to its own legitimacy. Like de Larosière before him, Camdessus understood and proved willing to accept the institutional risks involved in playing crisis manager in such a context. The world had changed a great deal since 1923, but his counterparts in the League would have understood the basic calculation.

For the Fund, decisions made in the Mexican case of 1995 had a shorter fuse but were not substantively dissimilar from those made since 1989 with respect to Eastern Europe and the countries of the former Soviet Union. In the aftermath of the collapse of the Iron Curtain, the organization had once again been assigned the task of crisis management. Camdessus clearly saw a role for the Fund early on. Internal studies on the monetary aspects of the transition from socialism were undertaken immediately after the first satellite states pulled away from the Soviet Union. The most authoritative discussions regarding the policy responses of industrial countries took place bilaterally and within the Group of Seven, but the Fund quickly began to feed its views through both channels. At the July 1990 G-7 summit meeting, the Fund was designated as convenor for the "Joint Study on the Soviet Economy," to be undertaken by the Fund, the

World Bank, the Organization for Economic Cooperation and Development, and the new European Bank for Reconstruction and Development.

Meanwhile, pathbreaking Fund stand-by arrangements were being negotiated with various Eastern European states. The first arrangements, with Hungary and Yugoslavia, were signed in March of 1990; Poland followed in May, Czechoslovakia in January 1991, Bulgaria in March, and Romania in April.[36] Later in 1991, a whirlwind of negotiations began with Russia and the other fourteen former Soviet republics. By May 1992, all had become members of the Fund. It was in the midst of this activity that the finance ministers of the G-7 met for formal discussions with representatives of Russia. On April 26, 1992, the ministers affirmed their commitment to provide a $24 billion "multilateral assistance package within the context of an agreed IMF program."[37] An initial (low conditionality) drawing of $1 billion followed in August as negotiations proceeded on a program for macroeconomic stabilization. Other drawings followed, many under the modified conditions built into a temporary new Fund program, the Systemic Transformation Facility established in April 1993.

In 1995, Russia was permitted to draw an exceptional amount in a bid to stabilize the ruble and advance the cause of reform. Behind that $6.4 billion lay the obvious preference of the leading member-states of the Fund not to take the financial and political risks of assisting the Russians directly. As in the 1980s in Latin America, the Fund was a convenient tool. Leading states obviously hoped that its use would simultaneously shield taxpayers in the West and promote reform in Russia. The deepest hope was that the situation could be "managed" during a long and treacherous transition at a time when the West had no political will to mount direct, massive assistance on the scale of a Marshall Plan.

In such a context, using the Fund had other advantages. Inside Russia, as in Mexico, the Fund could take the heat for painful social and political changes. The point was made clear in the 1996 presidential campaign when a spokesman for the Communist opposition to Boris Yeltsin declared, "Russia is losing its independence to carry out its international economic policy. . . . Its policy is not being decided by Parliament but by the IMF."[38] Less obviously, the Fund promised at least a partial buffer for Western governments. If the transition to capitalism in Russia ultimately failed, the Fund would play the most spectacular scapegoat role of its long career.

In the mid-1990s, there was much talk in the G-7 about the need for a new international facility capable of disbursing large amounts of emergency funding to countries facing sudden outward flows of capital. The design of such a facility in the Fund, and the stipulation of conditions on its use, was controversial. Opponents feared that its effective promise of a bailout for poor policy judgments would increase, not decrease, systemic instability. Others saw it as a weak substitute for the role now truly needed in a world of integrating capital markets, that of a real bankruptcy court for insolvent nations. But the latter course remained as politically unrealistic as it had been in the 1920s. A court above nations implied the existence of political authority above states. Just as no such authority had been capable of enforcing a timely resolution of the interwar reparations problem, so no such authority now was capable of enforcing international bankruptcy agreements. What did exist in the 1990s, however, was an organization of virtually universal membership possessing sufficient delegated legal authority to encourage collaborative national adjustment to a new international financial environment. That authority remained centered in the Fund's surveillance mandate.

In April 1995, the finance ministers and central bank governors of the leading members of the Fund met for their regular semiannual meeting in Washington. Reflecting on the latest Mexican crisis, the committee called for "stronger and more effective IMF surveillance of its members' policies."[39] In line with such objectives, the 1977 Surveillance Decision of the Fund's Executive Board was soon amended. To the traditional list of developments that trigger special discussions between the Fund and a member was added "unsustainable flows of private capital."[40] That seemingly innocuous phrase signaled a further expansion of the Fund's core mandate. Although it did not provide the formal jurisdictional scope of a revision of the Fund's articles, in historical terms it was a further step in justifying the Fund's increasing interest in the capital accounts, and not just the current accounts, of its members.

Building on that base, the leaders of the G-7 agreed in June 1995 to establish an emergency financing facility in the Fund that "would provide faster access to IMF arrangements with strong conditionality and larger up-front disbursements in crisis situations." [41] At its annual meeting a few months later, the Fund was enjoined by its industrialized members to use its new leverage to encourage countries to publish a wider range of useful economic information. Although the standards set by the Fund were to be voluntary, the goal was thereby to improve access to, and retention of, private capital. The IMF was also directed, "in the context of promoting broader market liberalization, to pay increased attention to capital account issues . . . and to give more attention to the soundness of financial systems." [42] Where its mandate had once been limited to promoting the restoration and expansion of trade flows, the Fund was now explicitly asked to advance the cause of enduring capital market integration.

The Expansion of Surveillance Mechanisms outside the Fund

As important as the finance ministers and presidents of leading industrial states make the Fund seem in the communiqués that often end their international meetings, they routinely forget about it when they design their own domestic economic policies. One statistic tells the tale. Ever since its surveillance mandate was formalized in the mid-1970s, the Fund has publicly and privately advised the members of the Group of Seven to restrain the growth of their fiscal deficits. Over the two decades that followed, their cumulative G-7 deficits (aggregate public debts) rose from 36 percent of their aggregate gross domestic products to 67 percent. [43]

It is true that during the 1980s, many G-7 members moved their monetary policies in the direction of the Washington consensus, but it would not be easy to prove that the Fund deserved much credit for this development. Nor was it self-evident that the expansion of international capital markets ever more closely monitored by the Fund caused this shift in their monetary policies. The easier case to make is that those markets helped them finance the consequences of their fiscal deficits, where there was much less consensus, while their monetary policies bore the brunt of their simultaneous and internally driven desire for lower levels of inflation.

Nevertheless, none of the industrial states evinced the slightest interest in downgrading the institution of economic surveillance itself. To the contrary, they embedded a surveillance mandate in a proliferating array of institutions. The mandate of the Fund became a model within the arena of trade policy.[44] On the Fund's own macroeconomic turf, leading states also came to rely on other organizations and informal forums with more limited memberships.[45] In the wake of the instability of the U.S. dollar in the 1970s, European states built their own regional monetary arrangements. By the 1990s, their plans for moving toward full-scale monetary union incorporated a surveillance apparatus like the Fund's, with the potential additional capacity to levy fines on member-states that violate agreed policy criteria.[46] At the same time, the major European states did not abandon the regular macroeconomic oversight discussions they had carried on since the 1960s inside both the Group of Ten and the Organization for Economic Cooperation and Development.[47] Among central bankers from the industrial countries, these discussions were complemented by regular meetings held in the forum of the Bank for International Settlements.

More prominently, Great Britain, France, and Germany, together with Japan and the United States, began holding their own talks on macroeconomic policy coordination as early as 1973. In 1986, the group was expanded to include Canada and Italy. Since then, the Group of Seven has become the premier forum for such discussions.[48] Despite its claim to institutional centrality in this field, the IMF had only a secondary role to play in the G-7.

In recent years the managing director has been invited to provide finance ministers at G-7 meetings with a summary of the Fund's current views on the condition of the international system and the requirements for stability. Over time, the ministers and their deputies have relied on the senior staff of the Fund for an increasing amount of technical assistance, particularly related to the use of comparable economic indicators to monitor and evaluate policy trends across the G-7.[49] But the Fund has never really been an intimate participant in the substantive policy discussions held privately among finance ministers or among their chief executives at the summit level. Not surprisingly, therefore, although enthusiasts for what came to be known as the G-7 process saw benefits coming from the informal or restricted nature of this alternative form of mutual surveillance, others saw few evident results beyond the slow erosion of broader norms of accountability, interdependent adjustment, and solidarity.[50]

The economic policies of the leading industrial states have the most significant implications for the world economy as a whole. With regard to those policies, plenty of room remained for skepticism about the actual utility of the Fund or of the surveillance instruments of other international organizations. Notwithstanding their own actions to create institutional competitors, however, the United States, Germany, Japan, and other leading states lost few opportunities in recent years to reiterate their solemn support for the principal mandate of the Fund. Indeed, in the wake of crisis after crisis, they turned back to that mandate and expanded it. Why did they bother? Were they simply hiring firefighters to handle emergencies, or priests to play the role of scapegoats? Or does multilateral economic surveillance, most fully elaborated and grounded in the Fund, help them address deeper concerns? The final chapter returns to the answer proposed in the opening chapters and examines it in light of the historical narrative.

CO CHAPTER 7

The Political Foundations
of Global Markets

*E*VEN TO THE CASUAL OBSERVER, IT OFTEN SEEMS THAT THE politics of financial policy, especially in modern democracies, centers around the avoidance of blame. To be sure, policymakers like to claim credit when it is there for the claiming, but they and their advisers often seem most concerned to ensure that they are not faulted when things go awry. In the Latin American debt crisis of the 1980s, in its aftermath in the 1990s, and in the financing of post-socialist transitions in Eastern Europe, the blame game was particularly obvious inside the leading states of the international economy. If developments went wrong, government officials could blame "independent" central bankers, central bankers could blame the IMF, and both could blame "the markets." The problem with this convenient formula is that modern markets do not run themselves.

Throughout the post–World War II period, the project of international financial integration has been led by the United States. After the broad restoration of currency convertibility in the late 1950s and early 1960s, other advanced industrial states embraced it, albeit with varying degrees of enthusiasm. Structural differences reflective of unique historical origins survived, but all advanced states widened and deepened the financial channels that, directly or indirectly, link their national markets. The project reflected a complex balancing of their own interests. It was not imposed, either by the United States or by the bankers. By the late 1980s, the prior decisions of leading states presented newly industrializing and developing states with an array of incentives to open their own financial markets—and a dearth of attractive alternatives.

All of the policies that had the effect of advancing financial integration came out of complicated internal processes of decision. But the collective result is beginning to make possible the international capital movements characteristic of the world economy before World War I. That potential has not yet been fully realized, except in a few stark cases like Mexico in 1994, but it is on the horizon. The trouble is that the political foundations that underpin increasingly integrated capital markets are no firmer today than they were in 1914, and in one basic sense they are weaker. It is that weakness which finally connects the experience of the League of Nations with that of the International Monetary Fund.

The Politics of Financial Integration in Retrospect

When open financial markets last formed the centerpiece of the world economy, a variant of the gold standard existed. As noted in Chapter 2, a modicum of internationally acknowledged rules of adjustment, and in effect policy coordination, then accommodated what economic openness was achieved. In principle, the capital flows generated mainly by trade were permitted to expand or contract national money supplies and thereby to influence national price levels. Internal price adjustments, in turn, potentially helped foster equilibria in national payments balances. In practice, the City of London's role as international creditor was at the center of the pre-1914 system and, when the system worked, British financing often eased the burdens of internal adjustment associated with expanding trade. Behind the City stood the waning commercial and military might of the British empire and the rising financial interests of American bankers like J. P. Morgan. That era came to an end in 1914.

The two decades following 1918 witnessed various attempts to recapture the now heavily romanticized virtues of a lost era. By accident and not by design, as we saw in Chapters 3 and 4, those attempts were associated with the League of Nations, then the only nearly universal political organization on earth. Beginning at Brussels in 1920 and Genoa in 1922, Great Britain and other leading members of the League attempted to recreate a set of agreed principles to guide economic behavior and thereby to reconstruct a world economy. The United States, necessarily in the shadows because of its failure to join the organization that had been the brainchild of its president, followed this attempt closely and did nothing to discourage it.

The embryonic economic staff of the League oversaw an effort to restore a functioning gold standard, a liberal trading system, and open capital markets. That this agenda was most compatible with the internal political and economic structures of Great Britain was no coincidence. In the early days, British nationals ran the League. Their interest in recreating prewar conditions remains perfectly apparent in the documents they left behind. Whether we interpret their efforts as nationalist, imperialist, or broadly internationalist, however, does not matter: it turned out that the old agenda could not accommodate postwar political realities, even in Great Britain. In the end, the League and its conferences proved inadequate instruments for fostering economic cooperation when domestic and international structures were in tumult.

Despite the lack of clarity of its economic and financial mandate, the League nevertheless recorded a few signal successes. League staff members played the role of financial crisis managers in Central Europe during the 1920s. Unlike the Fund, the League had no financial resources of its own. It nevertheless effectively coordinated the interests of foreign bankers and bondholders and those of a few heavily indebted states. At the very least, the League helped postpone their fall into the abyss of depression and war. In the Austrian case, for example, one could argue that it forestalled German intervention and

British and French countermoves. In this tangible sense, it provided leading states with a buffer. The IMF would perform a similar function many years later.

The League's success in Central Europe did not bring institutional reward. Indebted countries soon got the message that to call in the League was to admit profound weakness. Even if advice from League staffers was less of a blow to national prestige than direct intervention by another state, few welcomed the prospect. By the end of the 1920s, it was clear to the director of the League's Economic and Financial Organization that the League had no long-term future in crisis management. Years later, he concluded that the judgment had been right. Only if states decided collectively to move in the direction of world federalism would they routinely accept the constructive intrusions of a central monetary and financial institution.

Useful and frustrating as its buffering role had occasionally been, the League moved the focal point of its economic work in a different direction during the 1930s. Finally turning away from futile conference diplomacy after the abysmal conclusion of the 1933 economic meetings in London, the economic and financial staff of the League developed a first-rate analytic capacity. In embryonic form, the staff began to provide something resembling systemic oversight. Without a clear mandate and on a shoestring budget partly underwritten by the Rockefeller Foundation, some of the best economists of the day were enlisted. The methods and the analyses they pioneered did little to turn around a deteriorating international economy, but they were remarkable for their time. They established important precedents for the future.

A shift away from nineteenth-century orthodoxies was inherent in this new economic work of the League. Combined with core Keynesian insights just then in gestation, the new emphasis of League economists on employment policies and on the need for a systematically integrated model of the world *political* economy stand out. Most important, the message League economists took with them into their Princeton exile continued to resonate a half-century later: in the absence of a uniform monetary standard, the road to international economic prosperity had to be paved by the voluntary coordination of national policies. The openness required for stable and enduring economic growth on a world scale could rest on no other base. The automaticity of national policy adjustment promised by a restoration of the norms of the gold standard was an illusion.

League economists concluded, in other words, that when no indisputable norms of monetary behavior existed and wide scope for discretion in national policymaking prevailed, a political process aimed at discerning and championing the common good had to be put in place. They did not use the word "legitimacy," but they were wrestling with the same issues that political theorists would later associate with the deepening of economic integration in a world organized around nation-states. They could not reliably coerce coordinated adjustments in the macroeconomic polices that underpinned an interdependent global economy. In a world led by democratic states increasingly committed to the maintenance of economic as well as political security for their citizens, the legitimacy of global markets could not be divorced from the fundamental legitimacy of the state itself. Adjustments in national policies were required to sustain economic integration across political borders; they had to be crafted by states and accepted by a critical mass of their populations. The Tinbergen-Polak econometric work during the last years of the League produced a pioneering model of the world economy on this very basis.

In this respect, the incipient systemic oversight function of the League in its last years foreshadowed that of the IMF. Indeed, the experiences of the two institutions were directly linked through the careers of Per Jacobsson, Louis Rasminsky, J. Marcus Fleming, and, especially, Jacques Polak.[1] On one issue, however, the League economists of the 1930s differed from the Washington consensus that would later come to be associated with the IMF. They believed that liberalizing trading arrangements was a priority much higher than opening capital markets. In the event of conflict between these goals, a conflict Ragnar Nurkse in particular saw as endemic to the interwar period, they thought that controls on at least speculative capital flows should be deployed in order to avoid destabilizing exchange rates and thereby disrupting world trade.

The idea of policy coordination championed by the League in its last days was in the background at Bretton Woods. As noted in Chapter 5, however, the mainly American plan finally adopted was an attempt to encourage such coordination through a mechanism that combined automaticity with flexibility. The pendulum swung slightly away from national discretion. The final plan for the post-war monetary system meshed currency convertibility with fixed but adjustable exchange rates. It also meshed the right to impose capital controls with a presumption against their sustained use. The U.S. dollar, and the dominant U.S. economy, underpinned the system that evolved when the Bretton Woods agreement was finally implemented. But it was vitally important to a generation of policymakers that a broadly accepted international treaty provide the foundation for that system. The system as a whole was said to rest, much as in the ancient Roman sense, on the rule of law. In fact, it continued to rest on power. Power was not banished, only tamed to some extent. In practical terms, the norms of the treaty were set against the continuing ability of states to manipulate the value of their currencies. Some had more ability than others.

The Articles of Agreement of the International Monetary Fund were designed to fill the void at the heart of the international economy which the League of Nations had struggled to rebuild. The League's mandate for systemic oversight had never been explicit or strong; the Fund was supposed to become the objective arbiter of a truly multilateral system centered on coordinated adjustments in exchange rates. This was not quite how things worked out.

From the start, with only a few brief, painful, and ambiguous exceptions ranging from France in 1947 to Britain in 1976, the Fund was never central to international monetary policymaking in the industrialized countries. Over the entire postwar period, there was never any doubt about the real sources of power and enforcement in the system. Congresses and parliaments would have it no other way. But the *idea* of the rule of law, which the Fund represented from its inception, was still important, and more than the legalist ideology of the Americans, who influenced the organization more than anyone else, was at work. The specter of the 1930s haunted the minds of the system's real architects—the spokesmen for the states ostensibly centered on those same congresses and parliaments—as they redesigned the Fund's initially limited oversight mandate and labeled it "surveillance."

Certainly the United States and other leading states used that specter for tactical purposes, both internally and externally. But no historical evidence suggests that their spokesmen did not actually believe that monetary anarchy on the scale of the 1930s could easily return. As the history of the renegotiation and ratification of the Fund's Articles in the 1970s suggests, at a minimum the specter helped leading states to resolve dilemmas of common aversion. As it hovered in the background, they committed themselves more fully to the basic principle of Bretton Woods: they were accountable to one another for the external effects of their policies, effects most immediately transmitted through exchange rates. Embracing such a commitment was not easy, even in the United States, where a wary Congress worried about what it implied. The state remained the ultimate locus of legitimate authority, but shared perceptions of the 1930s pushed states toward the modest concession represented by the notion of formal accountability to the international community. The idea of Fund surveillance rested upon common memories of the bitter experience through which the League of Nations had lived.

The story of the collapse of the Bretton Woods system in the 1970s, and of the subsequent and rapid expansion of international capital flows, is well known. This book has emphasized one theme in that story. Widely shared perceptions of the 1930s caused the reconstruction of looser exchange-rate arrangements capable of accommodating those flows to involve upgrading and clarifying the oversight mandate of the Fund. The exercise was all about attempting to limit the room for national discretion in a politically acceptable fashion. From now on, the Fund was to provide "firm surveillance" of those policies of member-states which had external consequences. Exchange rates were freed from the formal strictures of the par value system, but an overarching environment of stability was viewed as vital. Legal commitments to avoid exchange-rate manipulation were duly reaffirmed, although it was broadly understood that only voluntary policy coordination across the leading economic powers could bring about the stability desired. This conclusion was, of course, exactly the one reached by League economists in the late 1930s. The analytic role they pioneered presaged the systemic surveillance work of the Fund after the Second Amendment.

In practical terms, the League had actually become a kind of think-tank in its last years. Especially with regard to the principal economic policies of leading states, did that too presage the ultimate role of the Fund in the contemporary period? The apparent interests of those states in the reconstruction of integrated capital markets suggest something more.

The Politics of Financial Integration in Prospect

A scholar of international financial relations recently offered the following reflection: "Financial markets, not states, represent the closest thing to a new hegemony in the contemporary international system. . . . A new Great Transformation will be required at a global, supranational level if values other than the establishment of a global self-regulating market are to be realized."[2] This is not an unreasonable position; indeed it expresses an argument that both liberals and radicals have long made. As I noted in Chapter 1, it also points to important distributional issues now becoming apparent even within advanced industrial societies. In international political terms, however, it can obscure more than it enlightens.

Contemporary financial markets may be blurring the traditional lines of international politics, but that blurring is still entirely reflective of dominant domestic political and economic structures and interests within leading states. Indeed, as discussed in Chapter 2, capital mobility and exchange-rate flexibility can in principle work together to advance those interests without compromising the abilities of such states to craft core policies autonomously. Once again, that combination of policies is the essence of international monetary arrangements that continue to incline toward integrated capital markets and away from fixed exchange rates.

For the leading states, policy autonomy is constrained only when they themselves embrace both capital mobility and some mechanism for fixing exchange rates irrevocably, as European states claim to be doing now on a regional basis. The same logic holds for other states, but a new source of vulnerability can arise from a high level of dependence on external sources of financing. Moreover, as Mexico discovered in the mid-1990s, the shorter the term of that financing, the more extreme is that vulnerability. In short, the international capital markets that provide greater flexibility to creditor states can severely reduce the flexibility of other states—other states that may one day become creditors themselves. Therein lies the ultimate rationale today for *multilateral* economic surveillance, a process of regular consultations, analysis, and consensus-building in a nearly universal forum. In such a forum, all states can become stakeholders in an economic system characterized not only by a presumption in favor of more liberal trading arrangements but also by increasingly open capital markets. Some will have more weight than others, but none will be excluded. The challenge is to ensure that the forum does not degenerate into an instrument by which the strong simply attempt to impose their will on the weak.

Once again, the same logic that led the League into a rudimentary form of surveillance—first through international conference diplomacy, then through special cases of national-level consultations, finally through scholarly analysis—has long been at work inside the Fund. When politics is bounded but economic aspirations are global, an institutional bridge is needed. To restate another metaphor used throughout this book, something has to buffer the interface between the politics and the economics. They do not mesh together naturally.

As members of the League discovered in the most painful way, the idea that a technical mechanism can be invented to force automatic, system-stabilizing policy coordination in a world whose political structure resembles our own is an illusion. In the early days of the League, that illusion took the form of the gold standard. In our own day, it takes the form of global capital markets. In a pinch, there remains no way to stabilize the world economy other than voluntary and adequately coordinated macroeconomic policy adjustments by leading states. This is the Achilles' heel of the financial integration project and the ultimate brake on its progress. Protecting that heel is the fundamental purpose of multilateral economic surveillance.

Recall the analytical framework inspired by Mundell and Fleming. Expanded international capital mobility can coexist with national political demands for policy autonomy as long as exchange-rate stability is given lower priority. After the collapse of the exchange-rate mechanism of the original Bretton Woods system, leading states—namely, the United States, Japan, and Germany—claimed to want both increased capital mobility and exchange-rate stability; to achieve those two goals, they claimed to be willing to give up a degree of autonomy by coordinating their macroeconomic policies. This, at any rate, appeared to lie behind the development and elaboration of the G-7 and other exclusive forums for discussion.

They obviously did not mean it in the 1980s, a turbulent decade marked by internal and external imbalances across the leading states. What they actually wanted was policy autonomy and capital markets open enough to finance imbalances, and that is what they got. In the 1990s, they attempted to address those imbalances once again, by voluntarily coordinating mutual adjustments in policy. Some success was achieved in the field of monetary policy, but fiscal policy remained a field impervious to external cajoling.

What objectives did other countries achieve during the decades after 1973? The answer is mixed. Heavily indebted developing countries certainly achieved an unattractive combination: openness to short-term capital flows that could destabilize even sound macroeconomic policies, instability in principal exchange rates, and little real autonomy. Similar pressures operated on industrial states with small, open economies, some of which effectively countered by giving up policy autonomy and pegging exchange rates to those of major trading partners. Others attempted in various ways to insulate their domestic markets from the ebb and flow of the most volatile types of capital flows. The question all confronted, however, was whether the power now effectively exercised through the capital markets was legitimate. Who gave the bankers increasing control over their policies? With less reason, but with a widening sense that something had indeed changed by the 1990s, such a question was even being asked in the United States, Japan, and Germany.

Unless the project of international financial integration is reversed, an unlikely and undesirable event, the question will continue to plague a world organized around states. And it is in that question that multilateral economic surveillance is now rooted. In the end, citizens continue to hold their own states responsible for the effects of capital market integration. The integration project is, however, an interstate project, spurred in part by a joint search for durable economic growth and in part by a mutual desire to avoid more difficult political choices. Multilateral surveillance is based on the principle that states are *accountable* to one another for the external implications of their internal policy decisions. Open capital markets help make those implications manifest. Multilateral surveillance is not based on the principle that states are *responsible* to one another for the content of those policy decisions. They remain responsible only to their citizens. This is what the debates over ratifying the reformed Article IV of the IMF Agreement were basically about. The distance between accountability and responsibility in this context is the difference between the IMF and global government.

In a world that shows little interest in the construction of global government, multilateral surveillance (whether located in the Fund or elsewhere) is an unlovely but feasible means of pushing the financial integration project in the direction of stable economic growth and shared prosperity. It is, however, a coping mechanism, not a solving mechanism.

Nothing can prevent powerful states from pushing financial integration in another direction, or indeed from moving away from it altogether. But only something like the multilateral surveillance instrument they have done so much to create can hold them accountable to one another. Since leading states have the most to gain from the integration project, and from the willing acquiescence of other states, it is ironic that since the 1970s they have risked discrediting it by holding their own most sensitive discussions about policy coordination outside its bounds. This is surely a mistake. By insulating themselves from criticism, and more important, from the need to explain and justify their system-shaping national policies in a more universal forum, leading states risk a great deal. As economic power disperses throughout the world, others may some day be willing to risk even more. Less distantly, the erosion of a credible forum through which those hurt by the integration project may seek redress and open-minded counsel cannot help but threaten the project itself.

Toward Global Markets?

The underpinnings of contemporary international financial markets consist, in a metaphor I used earlier, of foundations and plumbing: constructively interacting national macroeconomic policies are the foundations, and a modicum of convergence in national regulatory standards is the plumbing. Central bankers, bank supervisors, securities regulators, and accounting standards boards have a large role to play in reinforcing the plumbing, and lately they have been doing so quite actively. All of their work is for nothing, however, if the central organs of government responsible for macroeconomic policy in an expanding array of powerful states move in distinctly different directions. Such a movement would crack the foundations of "global" finance, and no superior force exists to fix it.

In principle, the creation and acceptance of a new gold standard or an alternative international regime of irrevocably fixed exchange rates might help constrain such a divergent movement. A revival of the more flexible exchange-rate mechanism of the Bretton Woods system might tend more gently in the same direction. No such scheme has even a remote chance of seeing the light of day as the twentieth century comes to a close. None has the slightest political momentum; neither does the equally chimerical idea of freely floating exchange rates combined with completely open capital markets somehow miraculously untethered from their political moorings.

At the end of the twentieth century, the macroeconomic policy coordination capable of sustaining increasingly integrated capital markets has to come through a convergence of basic interests within a widening array of states. An institutionalized and broadly representative process of information-sharing, consultation, and consensus-building does not guarantee such convergence, but it provides the only politically practicable tools. The pioneering work of the League presaged such a process; its contemporary manifestation in the IMF is a limited advance. On the one hand, the legal symmetry inherent in the Fund's surveillance instrument is important in a world where formal sovereignty still matters. On the other hand, the asymmetries in actual application reflect the realities of national and international politics.

Despite the ruminations of bankers about a new "information standard" ruling a borderless economy, the fact is that the currencies of the leading industrial states continue to provide the actual standards. Even in a world where traditional forms of capital control are ineffective, the economic policies of those states continue decisively to mold and shape integrating capital markets. Our collective prosperity depends on the successful management of the relationships among them.

The importance of the collaborative assessment and steering of national policy interactions will become even clearer if a solid European monetary union begins to flourish. With world monetary power more evenly balanced, the probability of exchange-rate and financial instability will rise. More intensive international collaboration will be essential. Under either flexible or managed exchange rates across potentially more cohesive currency regions, international capital flows will be no more capable of delivering "automatic" adjustment than they were in the 1920s.

Beyond the leading industrial states, future shifts in economic power will likely complicate the process of international adjustment. China and Russia, for example, are unlikely to surrender forever the degree of policy autonomy associated with the management of their own currencies. The markets that link such economies more strongly with others look set to rely on more inclusive, symmetrical, and effective forms of political collaboration. Unless such collaboration delivers reasonable stability and widening prosperity, even the citizens of leading states will rightly begin asking why they must defer to decisions over which they are losing control, and why the political authorities responsible to them are becoming impotent. At that point, the retreat from global markets will begin.

Ɛ᳒Ɔ

Notes

CHAPTER I
Global Markets and National Politics

1. Eric Helleiner, *States and the Reemergence of Global Finance,* Ithaca: Cornell University Press, 1994.

2. See, for example, Michael Sandel, *Democracy's Discontent: America in Search of a Public Philosophy,* Cambridge: Harvard University Press, 1996.

3. The analytical literature has an extensive lineage. Contemporary economic analysis begins with Richard N. Cooper, *The Economics of Interdependence,* New York: McGraw-Hill, 1968. Robert Keohane and Joseph Nye brought the subject fully into the arena of political science with their edited volume, *Transnational Relations and World Politics,* Cambridge: Harvard University Press, 1972, and later with *Power and Interdependence,* Boston: Little, Brown, 1977.

4. Ralph Bryant, "International Cooperation in the Making of National Macroeconomic Policies: Where Do We Stand?" in Peter Kenen, ed., *Understanding Interdependence: The Macroeconomics of the Open Economy,* Princeton: Princeton University Press, 1995.

5. In now standard usage, such institutions are "multilateral" if they aim to coordinate behavior among three or more states on the basis of generalized principles of conduct. Strictly speaking, coordination problems may be controversial but are often straightforward, for example, establishing standards for communication. Collaboration problems such as establishing free-trade regimes tend to be more complex; mixed motives may be common among interested parties, basic conflicts of interest may be apparent, and shared understandings of both problem and solution may not exist. See John Gerard Ruggie, ed., *Multilateralism Matters: The Theory and Praxis of an Institutional Form,* New York: Columbia University Press, 1993.

6. C. B. Macpherson elegantly sets out the contrasting visions of democracy at work here in *The Life and Times of Liberal Democracy,* Oxford: Oxford University Press, 1977; Eric Helleiner reintroduces Macpherson's framework to the study

of the implications of contemporary financial integration in "Democratic Governance in an Era of Global Finance," in Max Cameron and Maureen Molot, eds., *Democracy and Foreign Policy,* Ottawa: Carleton University Press, 1995.

7. See, for example, Ethan Kapstein, *Governing the Global Economy,* Cambridge: Harvard University Press, 1994.

8. John Goodman, *Monetary Sovereignty,* Ithaca: Cornell University Press, 1992; and John Woolley, *Monetary Politics,* New York: Cambridge University Press, 1984.

9. For a recent survey and analysis of the overarching policy context, see Michael Webb, *The Political Economy of Policy Coordination: International Adjustment since 1945,* Ithaca: Cornell University Press, 1995.

10. In the mid-1990s, the Brookings Institution sponsored a series of studies on "Integrating National Economies." Contributors were asked to write with a similar spectrum of possibilities in mind. Project leaders depicted a continuum of policy responses to pressures unleashed by increasing openness, ranging from national autonomy to mutual recognition of national standards and practices to decentralization to formal policy coordination to explicit harmonization, and finally to federalist mutual governance. On such a continuum, multilateral economic surveillance exists in the political space between monitored decentralization and formal coordination. See Miles Kahler, *International Institutions and the Political Economy of Integration,* Washington, D.C.: Brookings, 1995.

11. The term "surveillance" is at the center of an expanding body of political analysis and critical debate on modern industrial capitalism. See, for example, Stephen Gill, "The Global Panopticon? The Neoliberal State, Economic Life, and Democratic Surveillance," *Alternatives* 2 (1995), 1–49; and Christopher Dandeker, *Surveillance, Power and Modernity,* Cambridge, UK: Polity Press, 1990. My subject is more specific and empirically limited in scope, but the larger debate on the intrusiveness of the public sphere in what has traditionally been regarded in the West as private is relevant.

12. The issue is central to research in the field of international political economy. See Robert O. Keohane, *After Hegemony: Cooperation and Discord in the World Political Economy,* Princeton: Princeton University Press, 1984; and Robert Gilpin, *The Political Economy of International Relations,* Princeton: Princeton University press, 1987.

13. Stephen Krasner, "Compromising Westphalia," *International Security* 20, no. 3 (1995/96), 115–51; Hendrik Spruyt, *The Sovereign State and Its Competitors,* Princeton: Princeton University Press, 1994.

14. For key antecedents, see Robert Tucker, ed., *The Marx-Engels Reader,* New York: Norton, 1972; Max Weber, *Economy and Society,* ed. Guenther Roth and Claus Wittich, Berkeley: University of California Press, 1978; Karl Polanyi, *The Great Transformation,* Boston: Beacon Press, 1957; Fernand Braudel, *Civilization and Capitalism, 15th–18th Centuries,* New York: Harper & Row, 1982; Douglass North, *Structure and Change in Economic History,* New York: Norton, 1981; and

Charles Tilly, *Coercion, Capital, and European States, AD 990–1990,* Oxford: Basil Blackwell, 1990.

15. Henry Kissinger, for example, adapted the Weberian conception in his recent book *Diplomacy,* when he reflected on the age of revolutions in European history. "The more extensive the eradication of existing authority," Kissinger noted, "the more its successors must rely on naked power to establish themselves. For, in the end, legitimacy involves an acceptance of authority without compulsion; its absence turns every contest into a test of strength." *Diplomacy,* New York: Simon & Schuster, p. 655.

16. Usefully for our purposes, Thomas Franck adapts the Weberian conception and defines political legitimacy as the "quality of a rule which derives from a perception on the part of those to whom it is addressed that it has come into being in accordance with right process." As indicators for "right process," Franck proposes tests of determinacy, symbolic validation, coherence, and adherence to a normative hierarchy. See "Legitimacy in the International System," *American Journal of International Law* 82 (1988); and *The Power of Legitimacy among Nations,* Oxford: Oxford University Press, 1990.

17. This usage relates closely to contemporary sociological understandings of the concept of legitimacy as "not an abstract principle but an elaborated accounting theory that links situations and structures with collective purposes." George M. Thomas et al., *Institutional Structure: Constituting State, Society, and the Individual,* Newbury Park, Calif.: Sage, 1987, p. 36. Also see Martha Finnemore, *National Interests and International Society,* Ithaca: Cornell University Press, 1996.

18. As Harold Berman demonstrates in his magisterial study of the origins of the Western legal tradition, long before even the precursors of modern states existed, political legitimacy involved a much more direct and mutually constitutive relationship between the ruler and the ruled. By 1200, Berman contends, it was well understood that rulers had dominion because they had the right to establish law in their respective territories; it was also well understood that right was grounded in what the Romans had long ago called the "communitas." Resort to the divinity was required mainly to address the more abstract conundrum posed by the idea that sovereign rulers were subject to the "rule of law," not least in their relations with one another. *Law and Revolution,* Cambridge: Harvard University Press, 1983, pp. 292–93.

19. John Gerard Ruggie, "International Regimes, Transactions, and Change: Embedded Liberalism in the Postwar Economic Order," *International Organization* 36, no. 2 (1982); "Embedded Liberalism Revisited," in Emanuel Adler and Beverly Crawford, eds., *Progress in International Relations,* New York: Columbia University Press, 1991; and "Trade, Protectionism and the Future of Welfare Capitalism," *Journal of International Affairs* 48, no. 2 (1994).

20. William Connolly, "The Dilemma of Legitimacy," in Connolly, ed., *Legitimacy and the State,* New York: New York University Press, 1984, p. 227. Jürgen

Habermas put this dilemma near the center of contemporary social and political theory in *Legitimation Crisis,* London: Heinemann, 1976. Important and directly relevant contributions to the ensuing debate have come from a variety of paradigmatic perspectives. They include Ronald Rogowski, *Rational Legitimacy,* Princeton: Princeton University Press, 1974; John Breuilly, *Nationalism and the State,* Manchester: Manchester University Press, 1982; Charles Taylor, "Legitimacy Crisis?" in Taylor, *Philosophy and the Human Sciences,* vol. 2, Cambridge: Cambridge University Press, 1985, pp. 248–88; David Held, *Political Theory and the Modern State,* Cambridge, UK: Polity, 1989; Rodney Barker, *Political Legitimacy and the State,* Oxford: Clarendon, 1990; Philip Cerny, *The Changing Architecture of Politics,* London: Sage, 1990; and David Beetham, *The Legitimation of Power,* London: Macmillan, 1991.

21. Martin Carnoy, Manuel Castells, and Steven Cohen, *The New Global Economy in the Informational Age,* University Park: Pennsylvania State University Press, 1993; Ash Amin and Nigel Thrift, eds., *Globalization, Institutions, and Regional Development in Europe,* New York: Oxford University Press, 1994; Hans-Henrik Holm and Georg Sorensen, *Whose World Order? Uneven Globalization and the End of the Cold War,* Boulder: Westview Press, 1995; R. J. Barry Jones, *Globalisation and Interdependence in the International Political Economy,* London: Pinter, 1995.

22. This hypothesis is at the center of an expanding body of theoretical, empirical, and ethical research. See, for example, Helen Milner, *Resisting Protectionism,* Princeton: Princeton University Press, 1989; Ronald Rogowski, *Commerce and Coalitions,* Princeton: Princeton University Press, 1989; Jeffry Frieden, "Invested Interests: The Politics of National Economic Policies in a World of Global Finance," *International Organization* 45, no. 4 (Autumn 1991); Frieden, *Debt, Development and Democracy,* Princeton: Princeton University Press, 1991; and Cheryl Schonhardt-Bailey, "Specific Factors, Capital Markets, Portfolio Diversification, and Free Trade," *World Politics* 43 (1991); Helen Milner and Robert Keohane, eds., *Internationalization and Domestic Politics,* Cambridge: Cambridge University Press, 1996; and Brian Barry and Robert Goodin, eds., *Free Movement,* London: Harvester Wheatsheaf, 1992.

23. For recent and relevant data on nation-states as rising centers of political identification, see Ronald Inglehardt, Neil Nevitte, and Miguel Basanez, *The North American Trajectory,* Berlin and New York: Aldine deGruyter, 1996, esp. Figure 6-7.

24. Robert Cox makes the case for such mobilization in *Power, Production, and World Order,* New York: Columbia University Press, 1987.

25. Timothy Sinclair, "Passing Judgement: Credit Rating Agencies as Regulatory Mechanisms of Governance in the Emerging World Order," *Review of International Political Economy* 1, no. 1 (Spring 1994), 133–59.

26. For a useful theoretical treatment of the difference between the organizing principles of hierarchy and anarchy, see David Lake, "Anarchy, Hierarchy, and the Variety of International Relations," *International Organization* 50, no. 1 (1996), 1–33.

CHAPTER 2
The Political Economy of International Capital Mobility

1. *New York Times Magazine,* March 5, 1995, p. 58.

2. *New York Times,* February 2, 1996, p. 5.

3. See John G. Ruggie, "Third Try at World Order? America and Multilateralism after the Cold War," *Political Science Quarterly* 109, no. 4 (1994), 553–70.

4. See, for example, Stephen Krasner, *Structural Conflict: The Third World against Global Liberalism,* Berkeley: University of California Press, 1985. On the choice between differently sized groupings, see Miles Kahler, "Multilateralism with Small and Large Numbers," in John Gerard Ruggie, ed, *Multilateralism Matters,* New York: Columbia University Press, 1993.

5. Anne-Marie Burley, "Regulating the World: Multilateralism, International Law, and the Projection of the New Deal Regulatory State," in Ruggie, ed., *Multilateralism Matters,* pp. 125–56.

6. Manuel Guitián, "Rules and Discretion in International Economic Policy," *Occasional Papers,* no. 97, Washington, D.C., International Monetary Fund, June 1992.

7. Robert Mundell, "The Monetary Dynamics of International Adjustment under Fixed and Floating Exchange Rates," *Quarterly Journal of Economics* 74 (May 1960); Mundell, "The Appropriate Use of Monetary and Fiscal Policy under Fixed Exchange Rates," *IMF Staff Papers* 9 (March 1962); J. Marcus Fleming, "Domestic Financial Policies under Fixed and Floating Exchange Rates," *IMF Staff Papers* 9 (November 1962); Mundell, "Capital Mobility and Stabilization Policy under Fixed and Flexible Exchange Rates," *Canadian Journal of Economics and Political Science* 29 (November 1963).

8. For exceptionally clear expositions, see Benjamin J. Cohen, "The Triad and the Unholy Trinity: Lessons for the Pacific Region," in Richard Higgott et al., eds., *Pacific Economic Relations in the 1990s,* London: Allen & Unwin, 1993; Peter Kenen, *The International Economy,* 3d ed., Cambridge: Cambridge University Press, 1994, chapter 15; and Dominick Salvatore, *International Economics,* 5th ed., Englewood Cliffs, N.J.: Prentice-Hall, 1995.

9. During the past thirty years, economists have subjected the model to rigorous scrutiny. One important set of criticisms centered on the effects of relative changes in domestic price and wage levels, which could offset the benefits of flexible exchange rates. Another set focused on the complicating effects of high external indebtedness. See Harry G. Johnson, "The Case for Flexible Exchange Rates, 1969," in Robert E. Baldwin and J. David Richardson, eds., *International Trade and Finance,* Boston: Little, Brown, 1974; Jeffrey Sachs, "Wages, Flexible Exchange Rates, and Macroeconomic Policies," *Quarterly Journal of Economics* 94 (June 1980),

and W. M. Corden, *Economic Policy, Exchange Rates, and the International System,* Chicago: University of Chicago Press, 1994.

10. See Jacob Frenkel and Assaf Razin, "The Mundell-Fleming Model a Quarter Century Later: A Unified Exposition," *IMF Staff Papers* 34 (December 1987).

11. C. Randall Henning, *Currencies and Politics in the United States, Germany, and Japan,* Washington, D.C.: Institute for International Economics, 1994.

12. See Rogowski, *Commerce and Coalitions,* Milner, *Resisting Protectionism;* and Milner and Keohane, eds., *Internationalization and Domestic Politics.*

13. See Kenen, *The International Economy,* pp. 533–45.

14. Ibid., p. 537.

15. Jacques J. Polak, "Fifty Years of Exchange Rate Research and Policy at the International Monetary Fund," *IMF Staff Papers* 42, no. 4 (December 1995), 739.

16. Ralph Bryant provides an accessible overview of the economic debate in *International Coordination of National Stabilization Policies,* Washington, D.C.: Brookings, 1996.

17. Kenen, *The International Economy,* p. 544.

18. The literature on this topic is voluminous. See, for example, Arthur A. Stein, *Why Nations Cooperate: Circumstance and Choice in International Relations,* Ithaca: Cornell University Press, 1990; Kenneth A. Oye, *Economic Discrimination and Political Exchange,* Princeton: Princeton University Press, 1992; David A. Baldwin, ed., *Neorealism and Neoliberalism: The Contemporary Debate,* New York: Columbia University Press, 1993; and Janice Gross Stein and Louis W. Pauly, eds., *Choosing to Cooperate: How States Avoid Loss,* Baltimore: Johns Hopkins University Press, 1993.

19. Specifying the conditions under which one or the other outcome ensues is the task leading scholars have set for themselves in recent years. See Robert O. Keohane, *International Institutions and State Power,* Boulder, Colo.: Westview, 1992; John Mearsheimer, "The False Promise of International Institutions," *International Security* 19, no. 3 (1994/95); and "Symposium on International Institutions," *International Security* 20, no. 1 (1995).

20. See Jeffrey Frankel, "International Capital Mobility: A Review," *Papers and Proceedings of the Annual Meeting of the American Economic Association* (1991); Maurice Obstfeld, "International Capital Mobility in the 1990s," in Peter Kenen, ed., *Understanding Interdependence: The Macroeconomics of the Open Economy;* Martin Feldstein, "Global Capital Flows," *The Economist,* June 24, 1995, pp. 72–73.

21. For an expansion of this point, see Barry Eichengreen, *International Monetary Arrangements for the 21st Century,* Washington, D.C.: Brookings, 1994; and Eichengreen, *Globalizing Capital: A History of the International Monetary System,* Princeton: Princeton University Press, 1996.

22. For a recent survey, see Benjamin J. Cohen, "Phoenix Risen: The Resurrection of Global Finance," *World Politics* 48, no. 2 (January 1996).

23. See, for example, Helleiner, *States and the Reemergence of Global Finance;* Philip G. Cerny, "The Deregulation and Reregulation of Financial Markets in a More Open World," in Cerny, ed., *Finance and World Politics: Markets, Regimes and States in the Post-Hegemonic Era,* Aldershot, U.K.: Elgar, 1993; and David M. Andrews, "Capital Mobility and State Autonomy: Toward a Structural Theory of International Monetary Relations," *International Studies Quarterly* 38 (1994).

24. See, for example, Stephen Gill and David Law, "Global Hegemony and the Structural Power of Capital," *International Studies Quarterly* 33 (December 1989); Tariq Banuri and Juliet Schor, eds., *Financial Openness and National Autonomy,* Oxford: Clarendon Press, 1992; and Stephen Gill, "Globalisation, Market Civilisation and Disciplinary Neo-liberalism," *Millennium* 24, no. 3 (Winter 1995).

25. See, for example, Ralph Bryant, *International Financial Intermediation,* Washington, D.C.: Brookings, 1987. Informed by such premises, Steven Solomon gives a complementary and highly readable account of certain political implications in *The Confidence Game: How Unelected Central Bankers Are Governing the Changed World Economy,* New York: Simon and Schuster, 1995.

26. See, for example, Louis W. Pauly, *Opening Financial Markets,* Ithaca: Cornell University Press, 1988; Frances McCall Rosenbluth, *Financial Politics in Contemporary Japan,* Ithaca: Cornell University Press, 1989; Sylvia Maxfield, *Governing Capital,* Ithaca: Cornell University Press, 1990; John B. Goodman and Louis W. Pauly, "The Obsolescence of Capital Controls? Economic Management in an Age of Global Markets," *World Politics* 46, no. 1 (1993); and Andrew Sobel, *Domestic Choices, International Markets,* Ann Arbor: University of Michigan Press, 1994.

27. See, for example, Susan Strange, *Casino Capitalism,* New York: Basil Blackwell, 1986; Geoffrey Underhill, "Markets beyond Politics? The State and the Internationalization of Financial Markets," *European Journal of Political Research* 19 (1991); Tony Porter, *States, Markets and Regimes in Global Finance,* New York: St. Martin's, 1993. For a recent overview of the practical issues involved, see Richard J. Herring and Robert E. Litan, *Financial Regulation in the Global Economy,* Washington, D.C.: Brookings, 1995.

28. The concept of regimes, as scholars of international relations now conventionally use the term, is elaborated in Stephen Krasner, ed., *International Regimes,* Ithaca: Cornell University Press, 1983; and Volker Rittberger, ed., *Regime Theory and International Relations,* Oxford: Clarendon, 1993.

29. For debate on this point, see Michael Loriaux, *France after Hegemony,* Ithaca: Cornell University Press, 1991; Paulette Kurzer, *Business and Banking: Political Change and Economic Integration in Western Europe,* Ithaca: Cornell University Press, 1993; Geoffrey Garrett and Peter Lange, "Political Responses to Interdependence," *International Organization* 45 (Autumn 1991); Paul Pierson, "The New Politics of the Welfare State," *World Politics* 48 (1996); and Suzanne Berger and Ronald Dore, eds., *National Diversity and Global Capitalism,* Ithaca: Cornell University Press, 1996.

30. Sylvia Maxfield, *Governing Capital,* Ithaca: Cornell University Press, 1990; and Stephan Haggard and Sylvia Maxfield, "The Political Economy of Financial Internationalization in the Developing World," *International Organization* 50, no. 1 (1996).

31. On the domestic and international politics of the gold standard, its short-lived and partial restoration in the interwar period, and its analog in the early decades after World War II, see Giulio Galarotti, *The Anatomy of an International Monetary Regime,* Oxford: Oxford University Press, 1995; Beth Simmons, *Who Adjusts?* Princeton: Princeton University Press, 1994; Barry Eichengreen, *Golden Fetters,* Oxford: Oxford University Press, 1992; and Robert Triffin, *Gold and the Dollar Crisis,* New Haven: Yale University Press, 1960.

32. See, for example, Kenichi Ohmae, *The Borderless World,* New York: Harper, 1990; Richard O'Brien, *Global Financial Integration: The End of Geography?* New York: Council on Foreign Relations, 1992; and Richard J. Barnet and John Cavanagh, *Global Dreams,* New York: Simon & Schuster, 1994.

33. On the former, work directly relevant to international systemic questions extends from the classic statement of F. H. Hinsley in *Sovereignty,* New York: Basic Books, 1966, to recent perspectives offered, for example, by Stephen D. Krasner, "Sovereignty: An Institutional Perspective," *Comparative Politics* 2 (April 1988); John Gerard Ruggie, "Territoriality and Beyond: Problematizing Modernity in International Relations," *International Organization* 47, no. 1 (1994); Samuel Barkin and Bruce Cronin, "The State and the Nation: Changing Norms and the Rules of Sovereignty in International Relations," *International Organization* 48, no. 1 (1994); Alexander Wendt, "Collective Identity Formation and the International State," *American Political Science Review* 88, no. 2 (1994); and Janice E. Thomson, "State Sovereignty and International Relations: Bridging the Gap between Theory and Empirical Research," *International Studies Quarterly* 39, no. 2 (June 1995).

34. See Cohen, "Phoenix Risen," p. 270.

35. Robert Cox, *Power, Production, and World Order,* New York: Columbia University Press, 1987, p. 256.

36. Harold James, "The Historical Development of the Principle of Surveillance," *IMF Staff Papers* 42, no. 4 (December 1995). James's excellent recent history of the Fund fills in the institutional context. See Harold James, *International Monetary Cooperation since Bretton Woods,* Washington, D.C., and New York: International Monetary Fund and Oxford University Press, 1996.

37. In *The Reconstruction of Western Europe, 1945–51,* London: Methuen, 1984, historian Alan Milward describes the inefficacy of the Fund in its earliest days. The problem flowed most directly from U.S. policy, whose line was established as early as 1946 at the first meeting of the IMF in Savannah, Georgia. "I went to Savannah to meet the world," Keynes later recounted, "and all I met was a tyrant." R. F. Harrod, *The Life of John Maynard Keynes,* London: Macmillan, 1951, p. 639. The American concern with controlling the early postwar system—and protect-

ing the U.S. Treasury from unwanted liabilities—is also examined in the pioneering work on the politics of decision making in the Fund: Susan Strange, "IMF: Monetary Managers," in Robert Cox, Harold Jacobson, et al., *The Anatomy of Influence: Decision Making in International Organization,* New Haven: Yale University Press, 1973.

38. Susan Strange, *Sterling and British Policy,* London: Oxford University Press, 1971, p. 292. Also see Susan Strange, "The Meaning of Multilateral Surveillance," in Robert Cox, ed., *International Organisation: World Politics,* London: Macmillan, 1969.

39. Herman Schwartz surveys the latter literature in "Can Orthodox Stabilization and Adjustment Work? Lessons from New Zealand, 1984–90," *International Organization* 45, no. 2 (1991), 222–56. Also see Geoffrey Underhill, "Keeping Governments out of Politics: Transnational Securities Markets, Regulatory Cooperation, and Political Legitimacy," *Review of International Studies* 21 (1995).

40. Judy Shelton, *Money Meltdown: Restoring Order to the Global Currency System,* New York: Free Press, 1994.

41. See, for example, Walter Wriston, *The Twilight of Sovereignty,* New York: Scribner, 1992.

42. Manuel Guitián, "The Unique Nature and the Responsibilities of the International Monetary Fund," *Pamphlet Series,* no. 46, Washington, D.C.: International Monetary Fund, 1992.

43. In the case of the surveillance mechanism envisaged during the process leading to a fully functioning European monetary union, a system of fines for non-compliance with certain associated commitments was contemplated to reinforce the sanction of peer pressure.

CHAPTER 3
The League of Nations and the Roots of Multilateral Oversight

1. I have put the matter starkly, but it is certainly reflected in the scholarly literature. See, for example, G. John Ikenberry, "A World Economy Restored: Expert Consensus and the Anglo-American Postwar Settlement," *International Organization* 46, no. 1 (1992), 289–321.

2. F. P. Walters, *A History of the League of Nations,* London: Oxford University Press, 1952. The subject is also given short shrift in more recent histories: George Scott, *The Rise and Fall of the League of Nations,* New York: Macmillan, 1973; and F. S. Northedge, *The League of Nations: Its Life and Times, 1920–1946,* New York: Holmes & Meier, 1986. This is especially curious in light of evidence that economic factors were much in the minds of those whose ideas helped spawn the League. Norman Angell, for example, wrote extensively and passionately about the economic underpinnings of peace. It is also known that he had direct personal influence on

Colonel House and President Wilson. See Scott, *Rise and Fall of the League of Nations*, p. 17, and Norman Angell, *The Economic Functions of the League*, London: League of Nations Union, 1920. Angell was blunt about his agenda. He saw economic conflicts as contributing to past and likely future wars. He noted England's "special dependence" on an orderly world. He saw the power and authority over economic matters wielded by the Inter-Allied Economic Commissions during the Great War as contradicting the orthodox argument that rational guidance of economic forces was impossible. He insisted that if governments did not lead that process, then "great international trusts" would. He concluded that the way ahead lay in the construction of "super-national" authorities. For a recent political analysis of international organizations that includes a general overview of the work of the League, see Craig N. Murphy, *International Organization and Industrial Change: Global Governance since 1850*, New York: Oxford University Press, 1994.

3. Martin Hill, *The Economic and Financial Organization of the League of Nations: A Survey of Twenty-five Years' Experience*, Washington, D.C.: Carnegie Endowment for International Peace, Division of International Law, 1945, p. 15. (The 1945 version was released in mimeo form. The document is an extraordinarily useful and detailed memoir, apparently drafted at the behest of the Endowment in light of the then-raging debate over the structure of international institutions after the war. It was republished in book form by the Endowment in 1946.) Another useful reference, albeit one that covers only the early period, is Wallace McClure, *World Prosperity as Sought through the Economic Work of the League of Nations*, New York: Macmillan, 1933. McClure was a member of the U.S. Department of State, and his lengthy and exhaustively documented history ends just before the World Economic Conference of 1933.

4. Article 22 aimed to establish equal conditions for trade in territories placed under League mandate, while Article 23e, harking back to the principle of nondiscrimination codified in the Cobden-Chevalier Treaty of 1860, declared "equitable treatment for the commerce of all members of the League." See Arthur L. Dunham, *The Anglo-French Treaty of 1860 and the Progress of the Industrial Revolution in France*, Ann Arbor: University of Michigan Press, 1930, pp. 141–42; Barrie Ratcliffe, "Napoleon III and the Anglo-French Commercial Treaty of 1860: A Reconsideration," *Journal of European Economic History* 2, no. 3 (1973), 582–613; and Philip Cottrell, "Anglo-French Co-operation, 1850–1880," *Journal of European Economic History* 3, no. 1 (1974), 54–86. The original American draft of the Covenant included an amplification of the third of Woodrow Wilson's famous Fourteen Points: that every nation should be free to adopt and change its system of export and import duties and prohibitions, but "every such system . . . shall . . . as to the rest of the world be equal and without discrimination, difference, or preference, direct or indirect." Since no consensus could be reached on this principle, justification for the later economic activities of the League always rested on the Preamble of the Covenant, which highlighted the general objective "to promote interna-

tional co-operation and to achieve international peace and security . . . by the prescription of open, just and honorable relations between nations." Hill, *Economic and Financial Organization*, pp. 15–16.

5. For the reflections of Monnet and Jacobsson on the League, see Jean Monnet, *Memoirs*, London: Collins, 1978; and Erin E. Jacobsson, *A Life for Sound Money*, Oxford: Clarendon, 1979.

6. The largest of the League's technical arms, the EFO was distinct from, but in some ways complementary to, the separately established International Labour Office. By way of comparison, the staff members of the separate organizations for Health, Communications and Transit, Drug Control, and Social Questions never numbered more than sixty in total.

7. Attributed by Salter to, presumably, Nixon. See James Arthur Salter, *Memoirs of a Public Servant*, London: Faber and Faber, 1961, pp. 174–75.

8. Personal interview, Ottawa, August 11, 1992.

9. Prominent bankers and business leaders were mainly involved. Their reports were backed by studies commissioned from the most eminent economists of the day, including Gustav Cassel, A. C. Pigou, Charles Gide, and Maffeo Pantaleoni.

10. The involvement of the United States in the actual day-to-day work of the League is a story in itself. Suffice it to recall an anecdote related by Jacques Polak, who was on the staff of the League from 1938 to 1943. Strolling the cavernous halls of the League's headquarters one day just after his arrival, Polak came upon an office humming with activity. His curiosity piqued, he was later told what "everyone" knew. The office belonged to a permanent "adviser" to the League from the U.S. State Department. (The matter of departmental identities would later turn out to be important in terms of carrying over lessons learned, for the post–World War II economic institutions would be developed under the auspices of the Treasury Department.) Interview, Washington, D.C., September 19, 1994.

11. International Financial Conference, "Report of the Conference, Brussels, September 24, 1920 (Geneva, UN Library, League of Nations archive, 1920, Box 503, section 10a, doc. 473), p. 10.

12. Ibid., pp. 11–12. The conference also called for drastic reduction in expenditures on armaments, then still averaging 20 percent of national budgets.

13. Without a basis in "sound" domestic policies, "devaluation and deflation would be needed, but this could be disastrous. [We therefore] do not recommend any attempt to stabilize the value of gold and gravely doubt whether such an attempt could succeed. [We believe further] that neither an international currency nor an international unit of account would serve any useful purpose or remove any of the difficulties from which international exchange suffers today. Ibid., p. 13.

14. League of Nations, *Brussels Economic Conference, 1920: The Recommendations and Their Application: A Review after Two Years*, Geneva: Economic and Financial Section, 1922 (Geneva, UN Library, League of Nations document C.10.M.7.1923.II).

15. Hill, *Economic and Financial Organization,* p. 22.

16. In the 1922 Report, code words were often used to express core principles, much as the contemporary Fund surveys speak of "fiscal consolidation" and "monetary stabilization." But everyone understood what they meant and what principles lay behind them.

17. In addition to the matter of the attendance of nonmembers, Lloyd George was particularly chary of making the conference a League event. As he explained with some prescience before the conference: "[Some] think that the Genoa Conference should have been left to the League of Nations. I am a believer in the League of Nations. . . . Yet you must not run a thing like this too hard. . . . The League of Nations is in the making. You cannot make these things by written constitutions. You must create confidence in them; and confidence can only be created by achievement, and every failure . . . at this stage is a ruinous one. It is like the fall of an infant; it might result in a broken spine and the infant simply limp for the rest of its days." Quoted in McClure, *World Prosperity,* pp. 214–15.

18. If the plans of Britain's prime minister, Lloyd George, had borne fruit, the conference would have ratified a British commitment to the territorial integrity of France, French concessions on the issue of German reparations, and a joint European-American agreement on the financial reconstruction of the Soviet Union. In the annals of the interwar period, however, the conference stands out as a diplomatic disaster of the first rank. The profound ideological cleavage between the Soviet delegation and the main sponsors was by now undeniable, and the highly emotional issue of reparations poisoned the atmosphere. Most famously, the Soviet and German delegations seized the opportunity to take a side trip to the nearby resort of Rapallo and negotiate a separate peace. In the end, none of the critical issues was settled, and most were further complicated.

19. The liberal tone was not always as "orthodox" as commonly depicted. The report of the Economic Commission, for example, certainly pushed for the limitation of restraints on trade to the fullest extent feasible, but it reserved nice phrases for certain types of government intervention, including "the development of public works in aid of unemployment." In any event, unanimity was obtained on many but not all issues. A recommendation supporting the most-favored-nation principle in trading relations, for example, was not unanimously supported. See J. Saxon Mills, *The Genoa Conference,* London: Hutchinson, 1922.

20. See McClure, *World Prosperity,* pp. 213–14.

21. John Maynard Keynes covered the conference as a special correspondent for the *Manchester Guardian.* His contribution included publication of his first scheme for the restoration of a version of the gold standard. Essentially a gold-exchange standard with limited fluctuations in exchange rates permitted, and with back-up financing provided by the U.S. Federal Reserve, the scheme attracted attention but proved stillborn. Keynes would return to the same basic idea in 1942, and by then his audience, especially the Americans, would be more receptive.

Robert Skidelsky, *John Maynard Keynes: The Economist as Savior, 1920–1937,* New York: Penguin, 1992, pp. 107–8.

22. Against the backdrop of his famous critique of reparations, Keynes wrote, "We are asking Russia to repeat words without much caring whether or not they represent sincere intentions, just as we successfully pressed Germany. . . . We act as high priests, not as debt collectors. The heretics must repeat our creed. . . . Genoa, instead of trying to disentangle the endless coil of impossible debt, merely proposes to confuse it further with another heap of silly bonds. The belief that all this protects and maintains the sacredness of contract is the opposite of the truth." Ibid., p. 109.

23. Hill, *Economic and Financial Organization,* p. 35.

24. "In the conditions prevailing in the early twenties, there was little prospect of bringing about concerted action to promote freer and more equal trade. Those conditions were political, financial, and economic in character; and it is important to note that while the political organs of the League were endeavoring to establish security . . . and the Financial Committee was assisting in stabilizing the currencies and reconstructing the finances of individual European countries, there was no means—and no plan—for dealing with the economic [read, political] causes of the existing state of trade relationships." Ibid., p. 36.

25. Memorandum by F. Nixon, Economic and Financial Section, August 1922, League of Nations archive, Geneva, Section file s.123, doc. 16/2.

26. Salter, *Memoirs,* p. 175. For further relevant background and analysis, see Peter M. Garber and Michael G. Spencer, "The Dissolution of the Austro-Hungarian Empire: Lessons for Currency Reform," *Essays in International Finance,* no. 191, Princeton University, Department of Economics, International Finance Section, February 1994; and Rudiger Dornbusch, *Post-Communist Monetary Problems: Lessons from the End of the Austro-Hungarian Empire,* San Francisco: ICS Press, 1994.

27. Quoted in Scott, *Rise and Fall of the League of Nations,* p. 80.

28. Arnold Toynbee, *Survey of International Affairs, 1920–23,* Oxford: Oxford University Press, 1925, pp. 321–22.

29. Scott, *Rise and Fall of the League of Nations,* p. 80. Salter claimed that the push to accept the challenge came from Jean Monnet, then of the League's staff. Monnet believed that external military intervention by competing powers, with all of its unpredictable consequences, could be averted if the League grasped the reins of a quintessential collective action problem. Salter, *Memoirs,* p. 178. It is worth noting that Monnet's homeland had the most to lose if the territorial expansion of Germany, itself unstable, were the end-result of Austria's financial collapse. There is evidence, too, that the Assembly and Council of the League were moved by emotional pleas from Monsignor Seipel, then Austria's chancellor. Scott, *Rise and Fall of the League of Nations,* p. 81.

30. Ulrike Huber, "Österreich und der Volkerbund in die 20er Jahren," Ph.D. diss., University of Vienna, 1992.

31. An American from the Inter-Allied Reparations Commission, Roland Boyden, had almost been appointed in preference to Zimmermann. Salter later blamed Zimmermann's lack of diplomatic tact for exacerbating internal political conflict between the major Austrian parties. Salter, *Memoirs,* pp. 180–81.

32. See League of Nations, *The League of Nations Reconstruction Schemes in the Inter-war Period,* Geneva: League of Nations, 1945; also see Richard Hemmig Meyer, *Bankers' Diplomacy: Monetary Stabilization in the Twenties,* New York: Columbia University Press, 1970.

33. League staff were also involved in raising private financing for Greece and Bulgaria when those countries were faced with massive refugee inflows in consequence of local wars. They worked under the direction of the now formalized Financial Committee of the League, which consisted of officials seconded by the British, French, and Belgian finance ministries, central bankers, prominent businessmen, and private bankers from Switzerland and Holland. There were also frequent direct contacts between League officials and Montagu Norman of the Bank of England, Benjamin Strong and George Harrison of the Federal Reserve, Thomas Lamont and Dwight Morrow of J. P. Morgan, and others. Salter, *Memoirs,* p. 190.

34. I am grateful to Harold James for emphasizing this point in personal correspondence. On the Polish case and the more general phenomenon of states and creditors seeking to resolve debt problems outside the forum of the League, see Meyer, *Bankers' Diplomacy.*

35. Salter, *Memoirs,* p. 182. He added wanly, "The Financial Committee was attempting to alter its standard form of association with borrowing countries when the change in the general world situation made an advance upon these lines impracticable." Also see League of Nations, *Principles and Methods of Financial Reconstruction Work Undertaken under the Auspices of the League of Nations,* Geneva: League of Nations, 1930.

36. The reparations debate has been well documented and analyzed elsewhere. For relevant analytical and historical commentary, see S. V. O. Clarke, *Central Bank Cooperation, 1924–1931,* New York: Federal Reserve Bank of New York, 1967; Stephen Schuker, *American Reparations to Germany, 1919–1933,* Studies in International Finance, no. 61, Princeton University, Department of Economics, International Finance Section, July 1988.

37. Quoted from the minutes of the assembly, in McClure, *World Prosperity,* pp. 215–16. At the same time, as one of the delegates noted in debate, there existed "an astonishing paradox: as money becomes stabilized, economic crises arise. In Germany [for example] monetary stability had prevailed for two years, yet it was immediately followed by an economic crisis." Ibid., p. 220.

38. Ibid., pp. 217–18.

39. League archives include files dating back to 1920 (Box 503, classification 10a, 1920) for correspondence from the International Chamber of Commerce.

40. McClure, *World Prosperity,* p. 219.

41. Ibid., p. 222.

42. Ibid., pp. 225–29.

43. Ibid., p. 231.

44. Salter, *Memoirs,* pp. 198–99.

45. See, for example, Peter Temin, *Lessons from the Great Depression,* Cambridge: MIT Press, 1989.

46. Per Jacobsson, *The Economic Consequences of the League,* London: Europa, 1927, p. 53.

CHAPTER 4
The Transformation of Economic Oversight in the League

1. League of Nations, *Report of the Gold Delegation of the Financial Committee,* League doc. II.A.12, 1932.

2. Diane Kunz, *The Battle for Britain's Gold Standard in 1931,* London: Croom Helm, 1987.

3. Helleiner, *States and the Reemergence of Global Finance,* pp. 35–36.

4. McClure, *World Prosperity,* pp. 235–39.

5. The debate over the actual effects of such exchange-rate policies and the incentives for and consequences of cheating on agreed monetary arrangements in general continues. See, for example, Barry Eichengreen and Jeffrey Sachs, "Exchange Rates and Economic Recovery in the 1930s," *Journal of Economic History* 45, no. 4 (December 1985), 925–46; Kenneth Rogoff, "Can International Monetary Policy Cooperation be Counterproductive?" *Journal of International Economics* 18 (1985), 199–217; Kenneth Oye, *Economic Discrimination and Political Exchange,* Princeton: Princeton University Press, 1992; and Barry Eichengreen, *International Monetary Arrangements for the 21st Century,* Washington, D.C.: Brookings, 1995.

6. Quoted in Skidelsky, *Keynes,* p. 481. Also see U.S. Government, Department of State, *Foreign Relations of the United States,* vol. 1, 1933, pp. 673–74. On the underexamined domestic political roots of Roosevelt's position, see Barry Eichengreen and Marc Uzan, "The 1933 World Economic Conference as an Instance of Failed International Collaboration," in Peter B. Evans et al., eds., *Double-Edged Diplomacy,* Berkeley: University of California Press, 1993.

7. Ibid., p. 482. On such themes, a vast literature has developed, some of which focuses specifically on the 1933 conference. John Odell, for example, compared the bargaining strategies employed then with the Bretton Woods experience. He concluded that a given structure of international power may preclude certain extreme outcomes but still permit a wide set of outcomes. To explain the precise outcome of 1933, he underlined the importance of large swings in national market conditions, painful national experience that discredits prevailing policy ideas, and

international technical disagreement. See "From London to Bretton Woods: Sources of Change in Bargaining Strategies and Outcomes," *Journal of Public Policy* 8, no. 3/4 (1988), 287–315.

8. Salter, *Memoirs,* pp. 196–97. It is interesting to note that after Salter retired from the directorship of the EFO in 1931, he returned to government work in Britain and fell into the emerging Keynesian circle. On the great internal debate over unbalancing the government's budget, he apparently sided with Keynes as early as 1933. One of the key principles of League orthodoxy was evidently proving itself to be quite fragile, although in this case the British government itself continued to adhere to orthodox prescriptions. Skidelsky, *Keynes,* pp. 467–68.

9. Barry Eichengreen and Peter Lindert, eds., *The International Debt Crisis in Historical Perspective,* Cambridge: MIT Press, 1989.

10. Hill, *Economic and Financial Organization,* p. 71.

11. Ibid., pp. 71–73.

12. Alexander Loveday, "The Economic and Financial Activities of the League," *International Affairs* 17 (1938), 788–808.

13. There is one important difference between the two. The surveys were addressed to the world at large and they were hortatory. The *World Economic Outlook,* on the other hand, is meant to be a policy document, to be discussed for its lessons by the authoritative organs of the Fund, its Executive Board, and its Interim and Development committees, and to provide the broad framework for the full range of related policy debates.

14. Neil de Marchi, "League of Nations Economists and the Ideal of Peaceful Change in the Decade of the Thirties," in Craufurd D. Goodwin, ed., *Economics and National Security,* Durham: Duke University Press, 1991, pp. 143–78. Also see Jacques J. Polak, "The Internationalization of Economics: The Contribution of the International Monetary Fund," paper presented at Duke University, April 7–9, 1995; and Polak, "Fifty Years of Exchange Rate Research and Policy at the International Monetary Fund," *IMF Staff Papers* 42, no. 4 (December 1995).

15. The Foundation also provided the League with $50,000 for the study of the double taxation issue mentioned above. For full background, see de Marchi, "League of Nations Economists," pp. 153–55.

16. The volume was subsequently revised twice, mainly to take account of Keynes's *General Theory* and other work thereby stimulated. The final League version appeared as Gottfried von Haberler, *Prosperity and Depression,* 3d ed., Geneva: League of Nations, 1941.

17. Jan Tinbergen, *Statistical Testing of Business Cycle Theories,* vol. I: *A Method and Its Application to Investment Activity;* vol. II: *Business Cycles in the United States of America, 1919–1932,* Geneva: League of Nations, 1939.

18. On Rasminsky's role and its broader context, see J. L. Granatstein, "The Road to Bretton Woods: International Monetary Policy and the Public Servant," *Journal of Canadian Studies* 16 (Fall–Winter 1981), 175–76; A. F. W. Plumptre, *Three*

Decades of Decision: Canada and the World Monetary System, 1944–75, Toronto: McClelland and Stewart, 1977; and A. L. K. Acheson et al., eds., *Bretton Woods Revisited,* Toronto: University of Toronto Press, 1972.

19. Technically, the first and third were linked as parts I and II of the report of the Delegation. The second came out as Nurkse's work. League of Nations, *Report of the Delegation on Economic Depressions,* part I: *The Transition from War to Peace Economy,* Geneva: League of Nations, 1943; part II: *Economic Stability in the Post-War World: The Conditions of Prosperity after the Transition from War to Peace,* Geneva: League of Nations, 1945. Ragnar Nurkse, *International Currency Experience: Lessons of the Inter-War Period,* Geneva: League of Nations, 1944. Providing background for this work, the Fiscal Committee of the League published an analysis of the central debate concerning the advisability or not of unbalanced budgets during depressionary troughs. See League of Nations, Fiscal Committee, *Report to the Council on the Work of the Ninth Session of the Committee,* Geneva, June 12–21, 1939.

20. See Stanley W. Black, *A Levite among the Priests: Edward M. Bernstein and the Origins of the Bretton Woods System,* Boulder, Colo.: Westview Press, 1991, p. 58.

21. League of Nations, *Report of the Delegation on Economic Depressions,* part I: *The Transition from War to Peace Economy,* p. 14. The supporting analysis was also published in J. J. Polak, "The International Propagation of Business Cycles," *Review of Economic Studies* 6 (1939), 79–99.

22. Alexander Loveday, "Problems of Economic Insecurity," cited in de Marchi, "League of Nations Economists," p. 177. De Marchi, who convincingly develops this theme, notes that the idea was also explicit in the work of other League economists, like J. B. Condliffe. Haberler's, Tinbergen's, and Polak's business cycle studies moved in the same direction.

23. By 1942, Keynes had worked out a concrete proposal along these lines for an international clearing union. The union was to be founded on a code of conduct centered on nondiscrimination, convertibility, and symmetry in adjustment obligations between surplus and deficit countries.

24. League of Nations, *Report of the Delegation on Economic Depressions,* part I: *The Transition from War to Peace Economy,* p. 14.

25. Personal interviews: Rasminsky, August 11, 1993; Polak, September 19, 1994.

26. Hill, *Economic and Financial Organization,* pp. 3–4.

27. Salter, *Memoirs,* pp. 200–201. Salter concluded that the only real solution in the long run lay along the path of federation.

28. Something similar happened at the Bank for International Settlements. Pushed to the political margins during the depression years, its staff produced a number of useful studies on longer-term issues. See Hans Schloss, *The Bank of International Settlements,* Amsterdam: North-Holland, 1958; and Beth Simmons, "Why Innovate? Founding the Bank for International Settlements," *World Politics* 45, no. 3 (1993), pp. 361–405.

CHAPTER 5
Global Aspirations and the Early International Monetary Fund

1. Article 1 of the original Articles of Agreement of the IMF establishes the machinery for consultation and collaboration on international monetary problems. Article IV, section 4(a), quoted above, spells out precisely what collaboration means. With the Second Amendment of the Articles, this became Article IV, section 1: ". . . each member undertakes to collaborate with the Fund and other members to assure orderly exchange arrangements and to promote a stable system of exchange rates."

2. For an introduction to the legal literature on this topic, see Joseph Gold, "Duty to Collaborate with the Fund and Development of Monetary Law," in *Legal and Institutional Aspects of the International Monetary System: Selected Essays,* Washington, D.C.: International Monetary Fund, 1979, pp. 390–409.

3. Richard Gardner, *Sterling-Dollar Diplomacy,* New York: McGraw-Hill, 1969.

4. Granatstein, "The Road to Bretton Woods," pp. 177–85.

5. Art. IV, sec. 5(f) of the original Articles.

6. Gardner, *Sterling-Dollar Diplomacy,* p. 124.

7. Ibid., p. 127.

8. See Susan Strange, *Sterling and British Policy,* by the same author, *International Monetary Relations,* Oxford: Oxford University Press, 1976; and L. S. Pressnell, *External Policy since the War,* London: Her Majesty's Stationery Office, 1986.

9. Gardner, *Sterling-Dollar Diplomacy,* p. 142; also see Armand Van Dormael, *Bretton Woods: Birth of a Monetary System,* New York: Holmes & Meier, 1978; A. E. Eckes, Jr., *A Search for Solvency: Bretton Woods and the International Monetary System, 1941–1971,* Austin: University of Texas Press, 1975; John S. Odell, "Comment," in Michael D. Bordo and Barry Eichengreen, *A Retrospective on the Bretton Woods System,* Chicago: University of Chicago Press, 1993, pp. 182–86; and Raymond F. Mikesell, "The Bretton Woods Debates: A Memoir," *Essays in International Finance,* no. 192, Princeton University, Department of Economics, International Finance Section, March 1994.

10. Such calculated framing of choices is central to prospect theory, and a growing body of research applies it to political decision making. For an orientation, see Stein and Pauly, *Choosing to Cooperate,* chapter 1.

11. See G. John Ikenberry, "The Political Origins of Bretton Woods," in Bordo and Eichengreen, *A Retrospective on the Bretton Woods System,* pp. 155–82.

12. Art. XIV, sec. 2.

13. Art. XIV, sec. 4. To the extent that other members considered any further "pressures" for payments liberalization and movement toward currency convertibility at a pegged exchange rate feasible or desirable, Articles XIV and XV also

included sanctions provisions. In short, following Fund "representations" that particular restrictions could be withdrawn, persistent reliance on those restrictions "inconsistent with the purposes of the Fund" could lead to a declaration of ineligibility to use Fund resources and ultimately to a requirement to withdraw from membership. In practice, following a 1947 episode involving France, the Fund has typically eschewed such tactics. For background, see Joseph Gold, "'Sanctions' of the Fund," *American Journal of International Law* 66 (1972), 737–62. An amendment to the Fund's Articles, proposed in 1990, reopened consideration of such matters by providing for the suspension of voting and related rights for members in arrears to the organization. This "third amendment" was subsequently approved. For analysis, see John W. Head, "Suspension of Debtor Countries' Voting Rights in the IMF: An Assessment of the Third Amendment to the IMF Charter," *Virginia Journal of International Law* 33, no. 3 (Spring 1993), 591–643.

14. J. Keith Horsefield, *The International Monetary Fund, 1945–65,* vol. I, Washington, D.C.: International Monetary Fund, 1969, p. 85.

15. Ibid.

16. Ibid., pp. 108–9.

17. *IMF Survey,* September 1991, supplement.

18. On the importance of interpretation to international monetary law as it has developed over time, see Joseph Gold, *Interpretation: The IMF and International Law,* The Hague: Kluwer, 1996.

19. See Margaret Garritsen de Vries, "The Consultations Process," in de Vries et al., *The International Monetary Fund, 1945–65,* vol. II, Washington, D.C.: International Monetary Fund, 1969, pp. 230–35. For background, see Horsefield, *International Monetary Fund,* vol. I, pp. 311–15. On the importance of interpretation of the Articles (by the Fund itself) as a method for adjusting the Fund to changing circumstances, see Joseph Gold, "Continuity and Change in the International Monetary Fund," in *Legal and Institutional Aspects of the International Monetary System,* Washington, D.C.: IMF, 1984, pp. 393–96.

20. See Manuel Guitián, "Fund Conditionality," *Pamphlet Series,* no. 38, Washington, D.C.: IMF, 1981; Sidney Dell, "On Being Grandmotherly: The Evolution of IMF Conditionality," *Essays in International Finance,* no. 144, Princeton University, Department of Economics, International Finance Section, 1981; John Williamson, ed., *IMF Conditionality,* Washington, D.C.: Institute for International Economics, 1983; and Jacques J. Polak, "The Changing Nature of IMF Conditionality," *Essays in International Finance,* no. 184, Princeton University, Department of Economics, International Finance Section, 1991.

21. Garritsen de Vries et al., *International Monetary Fund, 1945–65,* vol. II, p. 241. The Fund's "scapegoat" role is the subject of innumerable anecdotes. One former finance minister from a developing country told me, for example, of an occasion when he specifically requested the managing director of the IMF to include in the routine surveillance report on his country a reference to the need to

cut military expenditures. At the same time, he told the managing director to expect a stinging reply from the country's president, a reply that he, the finance minister, would draft himself. The matter proceeded accordingly, and the ruse apparently achieved its objective of adding weight to the views of the minister, and deflecting blame away from him, during a crucial Cabinet meeting. Interview, Washington, D.C., May 19, 1994. For a more subtle example in an industrial country, see Otmar Emminger, *D-Mark, Dollar, Währungskrisen,* Stuttgart: Deutsche Verlags-Anstalt, 1986, pp. 85–88.

22. E.B. Decision No. 1034–(60/27), June 1, 1960. In this regard, the central question that gave rise to some disagreement was whether, like an Article XIV consultation, an Article VIII consultation should conclude with a Board decision putting forward an official Fund position on the affairs of the member concerned. In the end, the Board deferred to the sensitivities of members agreeing to engage in the consultations on an essentially voluntary basis. Unlike Article XIV consultations, no formal recommendations would conclude Article VIII consultations. But this did not mean that the consultations process itself would preclude constructive criticism concerning both the external and the internal policies of Article VIII members, however debatable the actual effects of that criticism.

23. Office of the Secretary of the Treasury, *Records of the National Advisory Council on International Monetary and Financial Problems,* Minutes, #62-1, Washington, D.C., National Archives, Box 3 of 61 (RG 56). The meeting was chaired by the secretary of the Treasury, with the chairman of the Federal Reserve, the chairman of the President's Council of Economic Advisers, and senior representatives from the State, Commerce, and other departments in attendance.

24. Ibid., attachment, p. 2.

25. Ibid., p. 3.

26. J. M. Keynes, "National Self-sufficiency," *Yale Review* 21, no. 4 (1933).

27. The view that all capital controls should be discouraged later became even more prominent in the American position, a development many students of the subject have attributed mainly to the resurgent influence of the New York financial community after the war ended. See Marcello de Cecco, "Origins of the Postwar Payments System," *Cambridge Journal of Economics* 3 (1979).

28. See Article VI, sections 1 and 3 of the Articles of Agreement of the International Monetary Fund.

29. Quoted in Joseph Gold, "International Capital Movements under the Law of the International Monetary Fund," *Pamphlet Series,* no. 21, Washington, D.C.: IMF, 1977, p. 11.

30. To take one example, note that leads and lags in current payments can effectively create "capital flows" which may or may not be equilibrating for a country's overall external balance. Controls on such flows have typically included a broad range of explicit restrictions, special taxes, or tacit arrangements designed essentially

to discourage certain kinds of financial transfers between residents and nonresidents. See OECD, *Controls on International Capital Movements,* Paris: OECD, 1982.

31. OECD, *Code of Liberalization of Capital Movements,* Paris: OECD, October 1986, Article l. Also see OECD, *Introduction to the OECD Codes of Liberalization,* Paris: OECD, 1987. Furthermore, the signatories agreed to "endeavor to extend the measures of liberalization to all members of the International Monetary Fund."

32. Code, Art. 3.

33. Ibid., Art. 7.

34. On the U.S. resort to controls, see John Conybeare, *U.S. Foreign Economic Policy and the International Capital Markets,* New York: Garland, 1988.

35. See Benjamin J. Cohen, *Organizing the World's Money,* New York: Basic Books, 1977; Fred L. Block, *The Origins of International Economic Disorder,* Berkeley: University of California Press, 1977.

36. See Helleiner, *States and the Reemergence of Global Finance,* pp. 102–11.

37. See John Williamson, *The Failure of World Monetary Reform, 1971–1974,* New York: New York University Press, 1977; and Fred Hirsch, Michael W. Doyle, and Edward L. Morse, *Alternatives to Monetary Disorder,* New York: McGraw-Hill, 1977.

CHAPTER 6
The Reinvention of Multilateral Economic Surveillance

1. This is certainly the testimony of one key participant, Paul Volcker. On this point, see his book with Toyoo Gyohten, *Changing Fortunes,* New York: Times Books, 1992. Also see John Odell, *U.S. International Monetary Policy,* Princeton: Princeton University Press, 1982; Joanne Gowa, *Closing the Gold Window,* Ithaca: Cornell University Press, 1983; Williamson, *The Failure of World Monetary Reform.*

2. Even those skeptical of the possibility of a depoliticized liberal internationalism concede the point and rightly emphasize that this was much more than an economic threat. It challenged a core element of the postwar U.S. attempt to address the international security dilemma. See Henry R. Nau, *The Myth of America's Decline,* New York: Oxford University Press, 1990, chapter 5.

3. E.B. Decision No. 4232–(74/67), adopted June 13, 1974. The Guidelines themselves were published in IMF, *Annual Report,* 1974, pp. 112–16. On decision making within the Fund in general, see Joseph Gold, *Voting and Decisions,* Washington, D.C.: IMF, 1972; *Exchange Rates in International Law and Organization,* New York: American Bar Association, Section on International Law and Practice, 1988; Stephen Zamora, "Voting in International Economic Organizations," *American Journal of International Law* 74 (1980), 566–608; Frederick K. Lister, *Decision-Making*

Strategies for International Organizations: The IMF Model, Denver: University of Denver/Graduate School of International Studies, 1984; and Kendall W. Stiles, *Negotiating Debt: The IMF Lending Process,* Boulder, Colo.: Westview, 1991.

4. For discussion, see Kenneth W. Dam, *The Rules of the Game,* Chicago: University of Chicago Press, 1982, pp. 196–99. It was significant that this was stated explicitly. Under the Articles of Agreement, Fund authority was specifically limited to restrictions on the current account. This tentative step toward extending that authority to the capital account in certain circumstances represented an important concession.

5. The agreement on gold also came down to a deal between the United States and France. The "demonetization" of gold, abandonment of an official price, and the disposition of the resulting capital gain on IMF gold holdings were the sticking points. Aware that the agreement was particularly important to France, the American Treasury secretary, William Simon, let it be known that the agreement would not be submitted to the Congress for final authorization until a deal was struck on the exchange-rate regime. Robert Solomon, *The International Monetary System, 1945–1976,* New York: Harper & Row, 1977, pp. 316–17.

6. For a fuller account and relevant references, see Louis W. Pauly, "The Political Foundations of Multilateral Economic Surveillance," *International Journal* 48, no. 2 (1992), 293–327; and James, *International Monetary Cooperation since Bretton Woods,* pp. 268–70.

7. F. Lisle Widman, *Making International Monetary Policy,* Washington, D.C.: The International Law Institute (Georgetown University), 1982, p. 52.

8. A plan for a return to pegged rates was embedded in what eventually became "Schedule C" of the Fund's amended Articles of Agreement. At the insistence of the United States, the text preserved the right of members to determine for themselves whether and when to return to greater exchange-rate fixity.

9. U.S. Congress, House, Subcommittee on International Finance of the Committee on Banking and Currency, *International Monetary Reform,* Hearings, 93d Cong., 1st sess., Washington, D.C.: U.S. Government Printing Office, November 13 and December 5, 1973, p. 22.

10. For further analysis, see Gold, *Exchange Rates in International Law and Organization,* chapter 9.

11. Article IV, sections 3 and 1 (iii).

12. U.S. Congress, Senate, Committee on Foreign Relations, *International Monetary Fund Amendments,* Hearings on S. 3454, 94th Cong., 2d sess., June 22, 1976, pp. 5, 27–33.

13. Looking back fifteen years later on the assumptions concerning floating rates widely held at the time, Paul Volcker labeled them "pretty naive." *Wall Street Journal,* November 28, 1988, p. A12.

14. See chapters by both officials in Jacob S. Dreyer et al., eds., *Exchange Rate Flexibility,* Washington, D.C.: American Enterprise Institute, 1978, pp. 181–90.

15. The Articles came into effect on April 1, 1978, following ratification by 60 percent of the Fund's members accounting for 80 percent of the total voting power.

16. Margaret Garritsen de Vries, *The International Monetary Fund, 1971–1978,* vol. 2, Washington, D.C.: International Monetary Fund, 1985, p. 840.

17. West Germany and France, in particular, retained the strongly held view that countries (read, the United States) should not be able to maintain exchange rates that had the effect of exporting inflation abroad.

18. The critical concerns of this group were that countries should defer to market forces and, in particular, that low-inflation countries should not be able to assist their export industries by resisting upward valuations in their exchange rates.

19. Decision No. 5392–(77/63), April 29, 1977, in IMF, *Selected Decisions* (15th issue), Washington, D.C.: IMF, April 30, 1990, p. 10. For analysis, see John H. Young, "Surveillance over Exchange Rate Policies," *Finance and Development* 14, no. 3 (September 1977), 17–19; and Dam, *Rules of the Game,* pp. 259–67.

20. On the logical inseparability of exchange-rate matters and other aspects of macroeconomic policy, see Richard N. Cooper, "IMF Surveillance over Floating Exchange Rates," in Richard N. Cooper, *The International Monetary System,* Cambridge: MIT Press, 1987, p. 149. On the basis of such reasoning, the Fund's surveillance mandate with respect to certain developing member-states expanded in a novel way in the 1980s. Procedures for "enhanced surveillance" were developed in connection with certain debt rescheduling operations. In this way, the Fund at times became a mediator between indebted member-states and international banks. See Joseph Gold, "IMF: Some Effects on Private Parties and Private Transactions," in Joseph J. Norton, ed., *Prospects for International Lending and Rescheduling,* Southern Methodist University Institute on International Finance, 1989, section 13.02[3]. Also see Benjamin J. Cohen, "Balance-of-Payments Financing: Evolution of a Regime," *International Organization* 36, no. 2 (1982); Garritsen de Vries, *Balance of Payments Adjustment, 1945 to 1986,* chapters 10–13.

21. On the implementation of the 1977 decision and its aftermath, see Eduard Brau, "The Consultations Process of the Fund," *Finance and Development,* December 1981, pp. 13–16, and David Burton and Martin Gilman, "Exchange Rate Policy and the IMF," *Finance and Development* 28, no. 3 (September 1991), pp. 18–21.

22. Joseph Gold, "Strengthening the Soft International Law of Exchange Arrangements," in Gold, *Legal and Institutional Aspects of the International Monetary System,* vol. 2, Washington, D.C.: International Monetary Fund, 1984, pp. 515–79.

23. See *IMF Survey,* May 22, 1995, pp. 153–56.

24. Economists call this a "liquidity problem" if it is short-term in nature but a "structural" or "solvency" problem if it is persistent and rooted in deep-seated internal inefficiencies. For background, see Peter B. Kenen, *Financing, Adjustment and the International Monetary Fund,* Washington, D.C.: Brookings, 1986.

25. Susan Strange, "IMF: Monetary Managers," in Cox, Jacobson, et al., *The Anatomy of Influence,* p. 272.

26. Joseph Kraft, *The Mexican Rescue*, New York: Group of Thirty, 1984, p. 5.

27. Volcker and Gyohten, *Changing Fortunes*, p. 205.

28. Ibid., p. 206.

29. Kraft, *The Mexican Rescue*, p. 46.

30. For amplification see Miles Kahler, ed., *The Politics of International Debt*, Ithaca: Cornell University Press, 1986; and Charles Lipson, "Bankers' Dilemmas: Private Cooperation in Rescheduling Sovereign Debts," *World Politics* 38 (October 1985), pp. 200–225.

31. U.S. strategic goals were certainly perceived in just such a light in principal European capitals. Background interviews, London, Paris, Bonn, May/June 1992. See Benjamin J. Cohen, *In Whose Interest? International Banking and American Foreign Policy*, New Haven: Yale University Press, 1986; and by the same author, "U.S. Debt Policy in Latin America," in Robert Bottome et al., *In the Shadow of the Debt*, New York: Twentieth Century Fund Press, 1992, pp. 153–72.

32. Solomon, *Confidence Game*, pp. 230–31.

33. This is the subject of a large, often critical literature. See, for example, Cheryl Payer, *The Debt Trap: The IMF and the Third World*, Harmondsworth: Penguin, 1974; Tony Killick, ed., *Adjustment and Financing in the Developing World: The Role of the International Monetary Fund*, Washington, D.C.: IMF and the Overseas Development Institute, 1982; Gerald K. Helleiner, ed., *Africa and the International Monetary Fund*, Washington, D.C.: IMF, 1986; Robin Broad, *Unequal Alliance: The World Bank, the International Monetary Fund, and the Philippines*, Berkeley: University of California Press, 1988; Jeffrey Sachs, "International Policy Coordination: The Case of the Developing Country Debt Crisis," in Martin Feldstein, ed., *International Economic Cooperation*, Chicago: University of Chicago Press, 1988; Tyrone Ferguson, *The Third World and Decision Making in the International Monetary Fund: The Quest for Full and Effective Participation*, London: Pinter, 1988; Joan Nelson, ed., *Economic Crisis and Policy Choice: The Politics of Adjustment in the Third World*, Princeton: Princeton University Press, 1990; Stephan Haggard and Robert Kaufman, *The Politics of Economic Adjustment*, Princeton: Princeton University Press, 1992; John Cavanagh et al., eds., *Beyond Bretton Woods*, London: Pluto Press, 1994; and Stephan Haggard, *Developing Nations and the Politics of Global Integration*, Washington, D.C.: Brookings, 1995.

34. Jacob A. Frenkel and Morris Goldstein, eds., *International Financial Policy: Essays in Honor of Jacques J. Polak*, Washington, D.C.: IMF, 1991. As made clear in a volume honoring Joseph Gold two years earlier, striking parallels exist in Gold's seminal contributions to the associated legal literature. See Joseph Jude Norton, ed., "Section's Tribute to Sir Joseph Gold," *International Lawyer* (special issue) 23, no. 4 (1989).

35. For analysis, see Moisés Naím, "Mexico's Larger Story," *Foreign Policy*, 99 (Summer 1995), 112–30; IMF, *World Economic Outlook*, Washington, D.C.: International Monetary Fund, October 1995.

36. See Mark Allen, "IMF-Supported Adjustment Programs in Central and Eastern Europe," in Georg Winckler, ed., *Central and Eastern Europe: Roads to Growth,* Washington, D.C.: International Monetary Fund, 1992.

37. *IMF Survey,* May 11, 1992, p. 151.

38. *New York Times,* May 7, 1996, p. A6. For more balanced analyses, see Anders Aslund, *How Russia Became a Market Economy,* Washington, D.C.: Brookings, 1994; and Randall W. Stone, "Russia and the IMF: Reputation and Unrestricted Bargaining," paper prepared for the 1996 annual meeting of the American Political Science Association, San Francisco, August 29–September 1, 1996.

39. *IMF Survey,* May 11, 1995, p. 129.

40. *IMF Survey,* May 22, 1995, p. 156.

41. *IMF Survey,* July 3, 1995, p. 203.

42. *IMF Survey,* October 23, 1995, pp. 314–15.

43. IMF, *International Capital Markets: Developments and Prospects,* Washington, D.C.: IMF, September 1994, p. 35.

44. On the Trade Policy Review Mechanism of the World Trade Organization, see Roderick Abbott, "GATT and the Trade Policy Review Mechanism," *Journal of World Trade* 27, no. 3 (June 1993), 117–19; Sven Arndt and Chris Milner, eds., *The World Economy: Global Trade Policy,* Oxford: Basil Blackwell, 1995; John Croome, *Reshaping the World Trading System: A History of the Uruguay Round,* Geneva: World Trade Organization, 1995; Petros C. Mavroidis, "Surveillance Schemes: The GATT's New Trade Policy Review Mechanism," *Michigan Journal of International Law* 13 (Winter 1992), 374–414; Victoria Curzon Price, "GATT's New Trade Policy Review Mechanism," *The World Economy* 14, no. 2 (June 1991), 121–37.

45. See Miles Kahler, "Organization and Cooperation: International Institutions and Policy Coordination," *Journal of Public Policy* 8, parts 3/4 (July–December 1988), 375–401; and Kahler, "The United States and the International Monetary Fund: Declining Influence or Declining Interest?" in Margaret P. Karns and Karen A. Mingst, eds., *The United States and Multilateral Institutions,* Boston: Unwin Hyman, 1990, pp. 91–114.

46. C. Randall Henning, "Economic and Monetary Union and the United States," in Manfred Weber, ed., *On the Rise of the European Monetary Union,* Darmstadt: Wissenschaftliche Buchgesellschaft, 1991; Michele Fratianni and Jürgen von Hagen, *The European Monetary System and the European Monetary Union,* Boulder, Colo.: Westview, 1992.

47. The main forum has been the regular meetings of Working Party 3 of the OECD's Economic Policy Committee. On the surveillance function of the OECD therein and generally, see OECD, *Interdependence and Cooperation in Tomorrow's World,* Paris: OECD, 1987; Emile van Lennep, *Fifteen Years of International Economic Cooperation,* Paris: OECD, 1984; OECD Economic Policy Committee, *Surveillance of Structural Policies,* Paris: OECD, 1989. Also see Robert W. Russell, "Transgovernmental Interaction in the International Monetary System, 1960–72,"

International Organization 27, no. 4 (1973), 431–64; Robert Solomon, "Forums for Intergovernmental Consultations about Macroeconomic Policies," *Brookings Discussion Papers on International Economics,* no. 15, Washington, D.C., Brookings, 1984; and Robert Wolfe, "The Making of the Peace, 1993: A Review of Canadian Economic Diplomacy at the OECD," Department of Foreign Affairs and International Trade, Economic and Trade Policy Branch, Working Paper, Ottawa, October 1993.

48. See Wendy Dobson, *Economic Policy Coordination: Requiem or Prologue?* Policy Analyses in International Economics, no. 30, Washington, D.C.: Institute for International Economics, 1991. Also see Robert Solomon, "Background Paper," in *Partners in Prosperity,* New York: Priority Press, 1991; Andrew Crockett, "The Role of International Institutions in Surveillance and Policy Coordination," in Ralph Bryant et al., *Macroeconomic Policies in an Interdependent World,* Washington, D.C.: IMF, 1989; I. M. Destler and C. Randall Henning, *Dollar Politics,* Washington, D.C.: Institute for International Economics, 1989; Robert D. Putnam and Nicholas Bayne, *Hanging Together: Cooperation and Conflict in the Seven Power Summits,* Cambridge: Harvard University Press, 1987; Yoichi Funabashi, *Managing the Dollar,* Washington, D.C.: Institute for International Economics, 1988; Robert D. Putnam and C. Randall Henning, "The Bonn Summit of 1978: A Case Study in Coordination," in Richard N. Cooper et al., *Can Nations Agree? Issues in International Economic Cooperation,* Washington: D.C.: Brookings, 1989.

49. Morris Goldstein, *The Exchange Rate System and the IMF,* Washington, D.C.: Institute for International Economics, June 1995.

50. See, for example, Fabrizio Saccomanni, "On Multilateral Surveillance," in Paolo Guerrieri and Pier Carlo Padoan, eds., *The Political Economy of International Cooperation,* London: Croom Helm, 1988; Catherine Gwin, Richard Feinberg, et al., *The International Monetary Fund in a Multipolar World,* New Brunswick: Transaction Books, 1989; Andrew Crockett, "The International Monetary Fund in the 1990s," *Government and Opposition* 27, no. 3 (Summer 1992); Eichengreen, *International Monetary Arrangements for the 21st Century;* C. Randall Henning, "Political Economy of the Bretton Woods Institutions," *The World Economy* 19, no. 2 (1996); and C. Fred Bergsten and C. Randall Henning, *Global Economic Leadership and the Group of Seven,* Washington, D.C.: Institute for International Economics, 1996.

CHAPTER 7
The Political Foundations of Global Markets

1. That linkage provides an interesting case for current analytical debates on processes of social learning and the roles of institutions in that regard. In short, it recalls the commonsensical but little studied idea that learning inside "epistemic

communities" requires teachers and agenda setters. It also gives substance to the old Weberian notion that the staffs of bureaucratic institutions embody collective memory. Weber pointed out that "central files" were important. Even more important, in this case, were individuals who, in a sense, helped create one set of files, personally carried them to another venue, and then helped succeeding generations interpret their holdings in a new context. See Emanuel Adler and Peter Haas, "Epistemic Communities, World Order, and the Creation of a Reflective Research Program," *International Organization* 46 (Winter 1992), 372; G. John Ikenberry and Charles A. Kupchan, "Socialization and Hegemonic Power," *International Organization* 44 (Summer 1990); John W. Kingdon, *Agendas, Alternatives, and Public Policies,* Boston: Little, Brown, 1984; Stephen Brooks and Alain Gagnon, eds., *The Political Influence of Ideas: Policy Communities and the Social Sciences,* Westport, Conn.: Praeger, 1994; and Finnemore, *National Interests in International Society,* chapter 2.

2. Philip G. Cerny, "The Dynamics of Financial Globalization: Technology, Market Structure, and Policy Response," *Policy Sciences* 27, no. 4 (1994), 339.

೮ふ

Selected Bibliography

Full references are included in the notes. I provide here a selection of accessible books for further exploration of themes highlighted in the text.

The linkage between international economic change and political legitimacy is enlightened directly or indirectly in William Connolly, ed., *Legitimacy and the State,* New York: New York University Press, 1984; Jürgen Habermas, *Legitimation Crisis,* London: Heinemann, 1976; Charles Taylor, *Philosophy and the Human Sciences,* vol. 2, Cambridge: Cambridge University Press, 1985; Stephen Krasner, *Structural Conflict: The Third World against Global Liberalism,* Berkeley: University of California Press, 1985; Robert Cox, *Power, Production, and World Order,* New York: Columbia University Press, 1987; David Held, *Political Theory and the Modern State,* Cambridge, U.K.: Polity, 1989; Thomas Franck, *The Power of Legitimacy among Nations,* Oxford: Oxford University Press, 1990; Rodney Barker, *Political Legitimacy and the State,* Oxford: Clarendon, 1990; Philip Cerny, *The Changing Architecture of Politics,* London: Sage, 1990; David Beetham, *The Legitimation of Power,* London: Macmillan, 1991; Martin Carnoy, Manuel Castells, and Steven Cohen, *The New Global Economy in the Informational Age,* University Park: Pennsylvania State Press, 1993; Beth Simmons, *Who Adjusts? Domestic Sources of Foreign Economic Policy during the Interwar Years,* Princeton: Princeton University Press, 1994; Hans-Henrik Holm and Georg Sorensen, *Whose World Order? Uneven Globalization and the End of the Cold War,* Boulder, Colo.: Westview, 1995; R. J. Barry Jones, *Globalisation and Interdependence in the International Political Economy,* London: Pinter, 1995; Helen Milner and Robert Keohane, eds., *Internationalization and Domestic Politics,* Cambridge: Cambridge University Press, 1996.

On the international political dimension of financial and monetary interdependence, see Benjamin J. Cohen, *Organizing the World's Money,* New York: Basic, 1977; Robert Keohane and Joseph Nye, *Power and Interdependence,* Boston: Little, Brown, 1977; John Williamson, *The Failure of World Monetary Reform, 1971–74,* New York: New York University Press, 1977; Fred L. Block,

173

The Origins of International Economic Disorder, Berkeley: University of California Press, 1977; Peter J. Katzenstein, ed., *Between Power and Plenty,* Madison: University of Wisconsin Press, 1978; Kenneth W. Dam, *The Rules of the Game,* Chicago: University of Chicago Press, 1982; Robert Solomon, *The International Monetary System, 1945–1981,* New York: Harper & Row, 1982; John Odell, *U.S. International Monetary Policy,* Princeton: Princeton University Press, 1982; Joanne Gowa, *Closing the Gold Window,* Ithaca: Cornell University Press, 1983; Susan Strange, *Casino Capitalism,* Oxford: Basil Blackwell, 1986; Benjamin J. Cohen, *In Whose Interest? International Banking and American Foreign Policy,* New Haven: Yale University Press, 1986; Richard N. Cooper, *The International Monetary System,* Cambridge: MIT Press, 1987; Robert Gilpin, *The Political Economy of International Relations,* Princeton: Princeton University Press, 1987; Ralph Bryant, *International Financial Intermediation,* Washington, D.C.: Brookings, 1987; John Conybeare, *U.S. Foreign Economic Policy and the International Capital Markets,* New York: Garland, 1988; Henry R. Nau, *The Myth of America's Decline,* New York: Oxford University Press, 1990; Richard O'Brien, *Global Financial Integration: The End of Geography?* New York: Council on Foreign Relations, 1992; Paul Volcker and Toyoo Gyohten, *Changing Fortunes,* New York: Times Books, 1992; Walter Wriston, *The Twilight of Sovereignty,* New York: Scribner, 1992; Philip Cerny, ed., *Finance and World Politics: Markets, Regimes and States in the Post-Hegemonic Era,* Aldershot, U.K.: Elgar, 1993; Tony Porter, *States, Markets and Regimes in Global Finance,* New York: St. Martin's, 1993; Richard J. Barnet and John Cavanagh, *Global Dreams,* New York: Simon & Schuster, 1994; Robert Solomon, *The Transformation of the World Economy,* Houndmills, Basingstoke: Macmillan, 1994; Judy Shelton, *Money Meltdown: Restoring Order to the Global Currency System,* New York: Free Press, 1994; Eric Helleiner, *States and the Reemergence of Global Finance,* Ithaca: Cornell University Press, 1994; Ethan Kapstein, *Governing the Global Economy,* Cambridge: Harvard University Press, 1994; Michael Webb, *The Political Economy of Policy Coordination: International Adjustment since 1945,* Ithaca: Cornell University Press, 1995; Jonathan Kirshner, *Currency and Coercion: The Political Economy of International Monetary Power,* Princeton: Princeton University Press, 1995; Steven Solomon, *The Confidence Game: How Unelected Central Bankers Are Governing the Changed World Economy,* New York: Simon and Schuster, 1995; Peter Kenen, ed., *Understanding Interdependence: The Macroeconomics of the Open Economy,* Princeton: Princeton University Press, 1995; Barry Eichengreen, *Globalizing Capital: A History of the International Monetary System,* Princeton: Princeton University Press, 1996.

On the domestic and regional politics of financial and monetary policy making, see John Zysman, *Governments, Markets, and Growth,* Ithaca: Cornell

University Press, 1983; Louis W. Pauly, *Opening Financial Markets,* Ithaca: Cornell University Press, 1988; Frances McCall Rosenbluth, *Financial Politics in Contemporary Japan,* Ithaca: Cornell University Press, 1989; Sylvia Maxfield, *Governing Capital,* Ithaca: Cornell University Press, 1990; Michael Loriaux, *France after Hegemony,* Ithaca: Cornell University Press, 1991; John Goodman, *Monetary Sovereignty,* Ithaca: Cornell University Press, 1992; Paulette Kurzer, *Business and Banking: Political Change and Economic Integration in Western Europe,* Ithaca: Cornell University Press, 1993; Andrew Sobel, *Domestic Choices, International Markets,* Ann Arbor: University of Michigan Press, 1994; C. Randall Henning, *Currencies and Politics in the United States, Germany, and Japan,* Washington, D.C.: Institute for International Economics, 1994; Stephan Haggard, *Developing Nations and the Politics of Global Integration,* Washington, D.C.: Brookings, 1995; Suzanne Berger and Ronald Dore, eds., *National Diversity and Global Capitalism,* Ithaca: Cornell University Press, 1996; David Andrews, "From Bretton Woods to Maastricht," manuscript; Kathleen R. McNamara, *Consensus and Constraint: The Politics of Monetary Cooperation in Europe,* Ithaca: Cornell University Press, forthcoming.

The politics of international economic policy coordination are treated in I. M. Destler and C. Randall Henning, *Dollar Politics,* Washington, D.C.: Institute for International Economics, 1989; Robert D. Putnam and Nicholas Bayne, *Hanging Together: Cooperation and Conflict in the Seven Power Summits,* Cambridge: Harvard University Press, 1987; Richard N. Cooper et al., *Can Nations Agree? Issues in International Economic Cooperation,* Washington, D.C.: Brookings, 1989; Wendy Dobson, "Economic Policy Coordination: Requiem or Prologue?," *Policy Analyses in International Economics* no. 30, Washington, D.C.: Institute for International Economics, 1991; Morris Goldstein, *The Exchange-Rate System and the IMF,* Washington, D.C.: Institute for International Economics, June 1995; C. Randall Henning, *Global Economic Leadership and the Group of Seven,* Washington, D.C.: Institute for International Economics, 1996. On the role of international organizations generally in this and broader contexts, see Robert O. Keohane, *International Institutions and State Power,* Boulder, Colo.: Westview, 1992; Craig N. Murphy, *International Organization and Industrial Change: Global Governance since 1850,* New York: Oxford University Press, 1994; Miles Kahler, *International Institutions and the Political Economy of Integration,* Washington, D.C.: Brookings, 1995; Richard J. Herring and Robert E. Litan, *Financial Regulation in the Global Economy,* Washington, D.C.: Brookings, 1995; Ralph Bryant, *International Coordination of National Stabilization Policies,* Washington, D.C.: Brookings, 1996.

On the economic and financial work of the League of Nations, see Martin Hill, *The Economic and Financial Organization of the League of Nations: A*

Survey of Twenty-five Years' Experience, Washington, D.C.: Carnegie Endowment for International Peace, Division of International Law, Washington, 1946; Wallace McClure, *World Prosperity as Sought through the Economic Work of the League of Nations,* New York: Macmillan, 1933; James Arthur Salter, *Memoirs of a Public Servant,* London: Faber and Faber, 1961. Complementary work includes S. V. O. Clarke, *Central Bank Cooperation, 1924–1931,* New York: Federal Reserve Bank of New York, 1967; Richard Hemmig Meyer, *Bankers' Diplomacy: Monetary Stabilization in the Twenties,* New York: Columbia University Press, 1970; Diane Kunz, *The Battle for Britain's Gold Standard in 1931,* London: Croom Helm, 1987.

The official histories of the International Monetary Fund written or edited by J. Keith Horsefield and Margaret Garritsen de Vries, as well as the forthcoming work of James Boughton, are important building blocks for research on the IMF. Coinciding with its fiftieth anniversary celebrations, the Fund commissioned a complementary one-volume study from an independent scholar. The result—Harold James, *International Monetary Cooperation since Bretton Woods,* Washington, D.C., and New York: International Monetary Fund and Oxford University Press, 1996—is an outstanding resource for those interested both in the Fund as an institution and in its broader place in the post-1945 international economy. Also useful are Joseph Gold, *Voting and Decisions,* Washington, D.C.: IMF, 1972; Robert Cox, Harold Jacobson, et al., *The Anatomy of Influence: Decision Making in International Organization,* New Haven: Yale University Press, 1973; Frank Southard, "The Evolution of the International Monetary Fund," *Essays in International Finance,* no. 135, Princeton University, Department of Economics, International Finance Section, 1979; John Williamson, ed., *IMF Conditionality,* Washington, D.C.: Institute for International Economics, 1983; Frederick K. Lister, *Decision-Making Strategies for International Organizations: The IMF Model,* Denver: University of Denver/Graduate School of International Studies, 1984; Peter B. Kenen, *Financing, Adjustment and the International Monetary Fund,* Washington, D.C.: Brookings, 1986; Joseph Gold, *Exchange Rates in International Law and Organization,* New York: American Bar Association, Section on International Law and Practice, 1988; Tyrone Ferguson, *The Third World and Decision Making in the International Monetary Fund: The Quest for Full and Effective Participation,* London: Pinter, 1988; Catherine Gwin, Richard Feinberg, et al., *The International Monetary Fund in a Multipolar World,* New Brunswick: Transaction Books, 1989; C. David Finch, "The IMF: The Record and the Prospect," *Essays in International Finance,* no. 175, Princeton University, Department of Economics, International Finance Section, 1989; Jacques J. Polak, "The Changing Nature of IMF Conditionality," *Essays in International Finance,* no. 184,

Princeton University, Department of Economics, International Finance Section, 1991; Kendall W. Stiles, *Negotiating Debt: The IMF Lending Process,* Boulder, Colo.: Westview, 1991; Manuel Guitián, "The Unique Nature and the Responsibilities of the International Monetary Fund," *Pamphlet Series,* no. 46, Washington, D.C.: International Monetary Fund, 1992; Paul Masson and Michael Mussa, "The Role of the IMF," *Pamphlet Series,* no. 50, Washington, D.C.: International Monetary Fund, 1995; Ian Clark, "Should the IMF Become More Adaptive?" *IMF Working Paper Series,* WP/96/17, Washington, D.C.: International Monetary Fund, 1996; Joseph Gold, *Interpretation: The IMF and International Law,* The Hague: Kluwer, 1996.

Index